ENGLISH ROYAL COOKBOOK

ENGLISH ROYAL COOKBOOK
Favorite Court Recipes

Elizabeth Craig

HIPPOCRENE BOOKS
New York

First published in 1953 by
Andre Deutsch Limited, London.

Originally published under the title "Court Favorites, Recipes From Royal Kitchens."

This edition published in 1998 by
HIPPOCRENE BOOKS
171 Madison Avenue
New York, NY 10016

ISBN 0-7818-0583-X

Cataloging-in-Publication Data available from Library of Congress.

Printed in the United States of America.

I GRATEFULLY DEDICATE
this book to that long line of Royal chefs
whose art made it possible. Their names may
not be quoted, but their fame lingers on
in their achievements.

CONTENTS

FOREWORD

EVER since I was twelve years old I have kept my eyes open for unusual recipes and interesting menus. When other girls were playing Snakes and Ladders, I was laboriously copying out recipes from magazines and newspapers.

Among them were various notes on royal fare, but it was not until about twenty years ago, when I met an Irishwoman who had the privilege of knowing an English princess interested in housewifery, that I began to wonder if some time in the future I might be able to make use of these.

One day this acquaintance, who had the privilege of dining with the Princess on an average once a week, asked me if I would like to have some royal recipes for my collection.

I replied: 'Do you really think this is possible?'

'Why not?' she answered. 'When I am dining with the Princess our conversation after dinner invariably turns to domestic subjects. She is very interested in them. Sometimes we discuss the favourite dishes of members of the Royal family, and sometimes the composition of the menus. She always insists that simple food is generally favoured.

'One evening,' she continued, 'shortly after dinner, the Princess asked me if I would care to see an old scrap book which had been given to Queen Victoria when she was a young girl. It had originally belonged to Princess Charlotte, daughter of George the Fourth and Caroline of Brunswick. Naturally I felt greatly honoured to have a peep at it. So, in the absence of her Lady-in-Waiting, the Princess herself went in search of this treasure, which had been bequeathed by Queen Victoria to a housekeeper.

'Hand-bound in vellum, with a crown stamped on every page, it was one of the most interesting volumes I have ever perused. Some of the recipes it contained were in old Italian handwriting. Others, equally difficult to decipher, as the pages were faded and spotted with age, were in print. From the dates one could tell that from time to time during the course of from fifty to eighty years these ancient recipes had been chosen and inserted with laborious care. There were "receipts", as recipes were then called, for dishes and wines,

9

A*

for the concocting of washes for the complexion, for perfumes, soaps, caudles and all the other fare and physic of bygone centuries. Many of them were in the girlish handwriting of Victoria the Princess.

'Then I was shewn another fascinating book of faded script, bound in Russian leather. It belonged to a member of the Royal Family. Within its covers I noted many recipes cut from old books and papers, alongside recipes evidently copied by Princess Victoria from some ancient, perhaps forgotten, books on domestic subjects. Amongst the latter transcribed in her sprawling unformed handwriting was a recipe for a plum pudding, dated 1565. On the first page of this beautiful little volume someone had penned the inscription "Given to Victoria on her birthday—1831." The entries in the book date from 1831 to 1887. Judging from the remainder of its contents other Royal princesses have added to this rare and valuable collection at later dates.

'My hostess told me, while I was eagerly scanning the precious volumes, that nearly every member of the Royal Family had a favourite dish or dishes. "The Prince Consort, husband of Queen Victoria, was German in his gastronomical tastes," she said. "He and the Baroness Lehzen hated one another very cordially, but in culinary matters they were absolutely united. Every week the Baroness used to receive big parcels of sausages, black bread, poppy seeds and almond sweetmeats from her relatives in Germany, and she always shared these good things with the Prince Consort. Indeed, very often when he was homesick, as he frequently was, she used to bake him German pancakes (*pfannkuchen*) and ginger-bread on the stove in her own rooms at Windsor. I sometimes think the Queen was a little jealous of the fact that the Baroness was so clever a cook. Her Majesty could not bear anyone to do anything for her Royal husband except herself. Dear Queen Victoria!"

'If I am allowed to copy out some of these recipes which have been handed down from generation to generation of Royal personages, some of which were already "old" long before the little Princess Victoria transcribed them, I shall, when I can, add notes about their history and origin.'

A month or two later I received a bundle of Royal recipes with the following note: 'I have copied out only the recipes which I thought you would find the most interesting. They are for your use by gracious permission of Her Royal Highness.'

This, briefly, is the story of the origin of *Court Favourites.* Now that all eyes are focussed on the British throne, and all thoughts are centred on the young beloved Queen, it seems fitting to introduce this collection to the world at large.

Hampstead, March 1953   ELIZABETH CRAIG

INTRODUCTION

COURT AND KITCHEN

EVER since mediæval times the Court has had a strong influence on the national kitchen. You have only to turn back the pages of history, and trace the evolution of the kitchen from feudal days, when it was the custom for all the inhabitants of a royal palace to dine together in the Great Hall, to the present moment, when any member of the Royal Family has only to express admiration for any new food or new dish to make it the fashion all over the Commonwealth, to realize how far food fashions at Court have always dominated fashions in the kitchen.

It is a far cry from the days of the Norman barons and from the Tudor and Stuart days when eating and drinking were so often carried to excess, and when every palace, castle and ancient keep had its vast kitchens where oxen and sheep were roasted whole, to the present days when most of us only eat to live: but if you care to browse over the growth of the British kitchen you will find that it has always been inspired by the Court.

Every sovereign has had some effect on national cooking, but none more than Richard of Bordeaux, son of the Black

Prince, for whose 10,000 courtiers and followers, 28 oxen and 300 sheep, besides a large number of fowls and a quantity of game, had to be daily prepared. A staff of two or three hundred cooks catered for their wants. It is said that King Richard died of hunger. This may be so, but while he lived, he earned the reputation of being 'the best and ryallest viander of all Christian kings', and we must thank his cooks, courtiers and doctors, who collaborated in inventing new dishes, hunting out unusual foods, and in treasuring recipes of tried favourites, for the basis of many national dishes for which England is still famed.

In Tudor days, the English Court entertained in a gargantuan fashion. Indeed so vast was the scale of entertaining carried on at Hampton Court that the Spaniards who came to England in the train of Philip the Second, severely criticised the number of kitchens and offices required to minister to the wants of the Court as well as the amount of beer consumed by the courtiers. But long before Henry the Eighth's day beer and wine flowed freely in England, and lavish feasting took place at royal and baronial boards. When Eleanor of Aquitaine was married to Henry the Second, it is recorded that a fleet of 200 ships was required to bring from France the wine for the celebrations. In those days, the art of brewing was still in its infancy, and wine was the royal beverage. It was not until the fifteenth century, so history relates, that brewing resulted in good ale. In Elizabeth's time, foaming bowls of ale seem to have been popular with courtier and commoner alike.

King Henry the Eighth was very particular about the maintenance of a public table at Hampton Court 'to which those at Court should without fail repair' as you read in the Ordinances of Eltham, prepared by Cardinal Wolsey for the regulation of the King's household. Led by bluff King Hal, the nobles throughout the country endeavoured to keep up this custom of communal dining. In ancient castles, great vaulted halls, situated over vast kitchens with huge, open fireplaces, still testify to the prevalence of this custom. The finest example of a kitchen of this kind is to be seen at Hampton Court where oxen were frequently roasted whole. The master-cook, dressed in satin and velvet, with a gold chain round his neck, would supervise his staff from a small room dividing the Great Kitchen.

Very long menus and heavy meals were the custom in the reign of Henry the Eighth. In those days, dinner was served at ten or eleven o'clock and supper at four or five o'clock, to the accompaniment of music, song, jest and stories. Led by the minstrels 'with pipes and drums, and tabours' the servitors carried the first course to the royal board, then wine and English ale flowed freely. It was only when a playwright or player pleased His Majesty mightily that a cup of 'Canary' or a draught of Rhenish wine was called for to pledge his health.

It was in the days of Queen Elizabeth the First that earthenware, metal and wooden plates came into general use at table. Before then rounds or squares of bread with the edges neatly cut, were baked and used instead. They were called plates or trenchers. Not until Charles the First sat on the throne did forks take the place of fingers, bifurcated daggers (from Persia *via* Italy) being the first form in which they appeared.

Mary of Lorraine, wife of James the Fifth of Scotland, introduced a French note to Scottish Court fare, and when Mary Queen of Scots returned to Scotland from France, this note became a song. Many moons have waxed and waned since those days, but the French influence still persists. We Scots claim that we have France to thank for much that is enjoyable in our fare, while England should be equally grateful to James the First for introducing the refinements of France to the English table. You can find many traces of the French influence not only in the names of national dishes to be met with north of the Cheviot Hills, but in the names of kitchen ware. One of the most striking examples of the latter is the Scottish name for meat platter which is 'ashet', derived from the French *assiette* meaning a dish.

The Tudors and Stuarts in turn dispensed regal hospitality. The fastidious palate of Queen Henrietta Maria, wife of Charles the First, was instrumental in introducing a more delicate note to the English kitchen. With the advent of William of Orange the character of the courses composing

English royal menus naturally changed, but it was not until Queen Anne ascended the throne that the art of cookery in England made much headway. Queen Anne, who in the words of a French author was *très Gourmande*, encouraged not only gastronomy but the art of wines. During her reign wonderful cellars were laid down in England. Unfortunately, Queen Anne's successors did not appreciate the good work she had inspired, and the character of our food suffered. George the First and George the Second both introduced a heavy Germanic influence, to the intense annoyance of Horace Walpole.

Queen Charlotte, wife of George the Third, who was very economical and disliked extravagance in any shape or form, did not help to improve matters. Yet she was most particular about how food should be cooked and her stillrooms at Buckingham Palace and Windsor were famous—or so says Madame D'Arblay in her diary. Although her table was by no means overladen, Queen Charlotte took a great interest not only in the preparation of food but in the herbs, fruit, and vegetables which were used in the Royal kitchens. It is said that she was so fond of mulberries that she greatly encouraged their culture. Some of the old mulberry trees in Buckinghamshire, it is claimed, were planted by this queen.

It was not until the close of the eighteenth century that any of the Georges showed real interest in the English table. Then the Prince of Wales, the future Regent, began to patronise the art of cookery and gastronomy. It required the arrival of the great Carême in the days of the Regency really to counteract the Germanic note in royal kitchens. When George the Fourth was King, Carême, who was his chef, laid the foundations of the modern dinner menu, setting and service. The national kitchen of today owes much to Carême's influence. He had a passion, however, for pictorial edibles: a passion, I am glad to say, which has not survived. Those works of art have vanished from modern tables as have the heavy *épergnes* beloved in Victorian and Edwardian days.

We have Horace Walpole to thank for a vivid description of a banquet given by the Intendant of Gascony to celebrate the birth of the Duke of Burgundy. It will serve to illustrate the type of table decoration then in vogue. The centrepiece he described was a group of wax figures moved by clockwork. At the end of the feast, the group was set in motion to give a representation of the labour of the Dauphiness and the happy birth of the heir to the monarchy.

King George the Fifth and Queen Mary are chiefly responsible for the simplicity of the English Royal kitchen of today. Both averse to elaborate dishes, they brought up all the members of their family to enjoy simple food. The meals served at Buckingham Palace, Sandringham, Windsor Castle and Balmoral during their reign were not the elaborate affairs one would fancy, except in the case of state or semi-state banquets. The menus for the family meals were generally short and consisted of simple dishes.

The Duke of Windsor has always been spartan in his tastes. Monsieur Herbodeau, the famous French master-chef, once sorrowfully remarked to me when he was reigning at the Ritz: 'He eats so leetle. A *filet de sole* or a *côtelette*. That is all. It breaks my heart.' It is said that when the Duke attended balls he never took any supper, even when he escorted his hostess. Once, when present at a banquet at the Mansion House, he gave the Lord Mayor an anxious time by passing course after course. At last, unable to ignore this any longer, the Lord Mayor said: 'Is there anything else you would prefer?' 'Could I have some cold ham?' was the reply. This does not mean that the Duke of Windsor does not understand food or is not interested in it. Several of the dishes we enjoyed at English tables before the war owed their presence on our menus to the interest taken by him in local fare when, as Prince of Wales, he made his tours of the Empire. Toheroa (pronounced 'Tokeroa') is a shining example. When the Prince visited New Zealand, he enjoyed Toheroa Soup so much that New Zealand was prompted to introduce this delicacy to England. It was quickly followed by savouries made partly from Toheroa paste, manufactured in England from this little New Zealand fish which is a distant cousin of an oyster.

The Duke of Windsor is not the only member of the British Royal family who has started a new fashion in food in Britain. When the Duke of Gloucester returned from one of his game-hunting expeditions, lion chops suddenly appeared on the menus of smart London restaurants, with the note: 'To order only. Time: Six weeks.'

King George the Sixth also preferred simple food. When not entertaining, Queen Elizabeth, the Queen Mother, favours menus usually composed of English and Scotch dishes. Scotch broth, Scotch salmon, roast venison, *noisettes* of venison, roast grouse, Scotch collops (commonly called 'mince' north of the Tweed), and Scotch mutton pies, I am told, figure from time to time on her lunch and dinner menus, while Scotch scones, shortbread, Dundee cake, and other Scotch tea breads made by her Scottish cook, often have pride of place on her tea table. One of the most popular meat dishes with both Their Majesties, the Queen Mother and the late King, and one which was sometimes served to Scottish friends when invited to lunch, was Scotch collops with a poached egg on top. The Queen Mother is a very careful housekeeper. She insists on the fullest use being made of British fruit, vegetables and all home products. Unlike many British housewives, she does not despise homely vegetables. No cook in the Royal household dare say to her Royal mistress, as many a cook says to mistresses of less important households, that carrots, turnips or any of the common vegetables are not good enough for the dining-room. She permits no snobbery in the kitchen.

It is a long stretch from the days when the ancient Britons lived almost solely on honey, milk, wild fowl and vegetables to the present day when canned, frozen and packaged food provide so much of our daily meals. Our diet down the ages has suffered many changes. As the members of the reigning Royal family have always influenced and sometimes inspired our national cooking, I feel sure that our young Queen, who took lessons in cookery, will lead us to fresh triumphs in the art of cookery and gastronomy. Although she eats very lightly, she knows more about the importance of good food than has done any other Queen of these islands. In the days to come Her Majesty, Queen Elizabeth, may help us to witness a renaissance in the culinary world. It is long overdue.

TO THOSE
WHO WISH TO TRY OUT
THE RECIPES

MANY of these recipes, you will find, leave part of their method to the imagination. They take for granted that those who wish to follow them know the basic methods of cookery. I could have rewritten them, but felt that bringing them up-to-date would spoil their character. When editing them, I only made such alterations as seemed strictly necessary. When I have inserted comments of my own they are given in square brackets, or in italics at the end of the recipe. In all the recipes measurements given are level.

E.C.

ENGLISH ROYAL COOKBOOK

SOUPS

FEW members of the Royal family have had their names associated with soups, particularly with soups popular in the present day. Queen Victoria and Prince Albert are the exception. When Prince Albert paid his first visit to the Highlands of Scotland, he developed a great fondness for hotch potch, a mutton and vegetable broth. It is a soup you have to taste in Scotland to find perfectly made. The English version usually contains barley. The Prince, it is said, when on Deeside, made its acquaintance on the slopes of a hill where he saw a herd-laddie supping it from a can. (I was reared on the belief that it was Queen Victoria of whom the story is told.)

'What are you having for dinner?' the lad was asked.

'Hotch potch.'

'What is hotch potch?'

'There's carrots intil't, neeps intil't, peas intil't, cabbage intil't.'

'Yes,' he was stopped, 'but what's "intil't"?'

'There's carrots intil't, neeps intil't,' and so on. It was not until a ghillie arrived and explained that 'intil't' meant 'in it' or 'into it' that the recipe was understood. You will find a simpler version of this soup on page 26.

QUEEN VICTORIA'S CHICKEN BROTH
c. 1853

1 boiling fowl
3 pints chicken stock
1 hard-boiled egg
1 teaspoon ground almonds
2 dessertspoons cornflour
½ pint milk
Salt and pepper to taste
1½ teaspoons minced parsley

Place a fowl with giblets and a small peeled onion, a prepared
and sliced carrot, a stalk of celery, sprig of parsley, six white
peppercorns, and cold water to cover, in a saucepan. Bring to
boil. Skim. Cover and simmer gently till bird is tender.
Strain off stock. Leave till cold, then skim off fat. Remove
meat from chicken carcase and mince. Rub egg yolk through
a sieve into a basin. Stir in almonds. Mince egg white. Mix
with the chicken. Dissolve cornflour in a little of the milk.
Add remainder of milk. Stir by degrees into the almonds and
egg yolk. Heat stock. Stir in cornflour mixture. Boil for
three minutes, stirring constantly. Remove pan from stove.
Stir in minced chicken and egg white. Reheat but do not
allow to boil. Season to taste with salt and pepper. Sprinkle
with the parsley.

QUEEN VICTORIA'S
CREAM OF CHICKEN *c.* 1844

3 fat chickens
Strong veal stock
3 sprigs parsley
2 tablespoons breadcrumbs
4 hard-boiled egg yolks
1 quart boiled cream
Salt and pepper to taste

Skin and clean birds. Wash them thoroughly in warm water.
Drain and place in a saucepan. Cover with veal stock. Add

parsley. Cover. Simmer gently till tender. Remove meat from their bones. Soak crumbs in half a cup of the stock for ten minutes. Chop meat. Pound it in a mortar. Stir in crumbs and egg yolks. Strain remainder of stock into a saucepan. Gradually stir in cream, then gradually stir in chicken purée. When blended, rub through a fine hair sieve. Reheat, stirring constantly, but do not allow to boil. Season with salt and pepper to taste. Serve with sippets of toast or with fried diced bread.

'THE ONLY SOUP EVER EATEN BY QUEEN VICTORIA' *c.* 1873

Francatelli, Queen Victoria's chef, says the following recipe is the recipe for 'The only soup ever eaten by Queen Victoria.' Perhaps this is true when she was in residence in England. The people of Deeside, Aberdeenshire, insist that she often ordered cream of chicken and rich chicken broth when living at Balmoral. The recipe for this 'Only Soup' was written in the manuscript book I mentioned.

Wash and scald half a handful of Frankfurt barley, put into a stew pan with three pints of good white veal stock and simmer over slow heat for one and a half hours when barley will be nearly tender. Remove a third of the soup into a small saucepan. Rub remainder through a hair sieve, and pour it on to the unsieved. Add half a pint of cream gradually, stirring constantly. Season with salt. Stir over stove till hot, then serve.

Francatelli also says that rice can be substituted for barley, but that it won't require so much cooking. E.C.

BLUE PEA SOUP *c.* 1735

Place three pints of blue peas in a pan that will hold about six quarts. Cover with rain water and place pan on a slow fire. Simmer till the peas are broken then mash them and add three or four quarts of water, six or eight onions, a few cloves, black pepper, half an ounce Jamaica pepper, one pound of bacon, a little thyme, a little dried mint, and three or four stalks of celery. [Save the best of the celery to boil as a vegetable, or to eat with cheese.] Boil soup till onions are tender and soup tastes nicely of bacon, then strain. Serve with cubes of fried bread.

HOTCH POTCH c. 1850

2 lbs neck of mutton
2½ quarts water
6 young scraped carrots
6 small peeled turnips
6 small peeled onions
2 pints shelled peas
1 small cabbage
1 small cauliflower
2 sprigs of parsley
Salt and pepper to taste

Trim and divide meat into chops. Measure water into a saucepan. Bring to the boil. Add trimmings of the meat, chine bone and salt. Boil for a moment or two, then skim carefully. Cover and simmer for one hour. Strain off stock into another pan. Add chops. Dice carrots and turnips. Chop onions. Add prepared vegetables to stock, then half the peas. Cover and bring to simmering point. Simmer for half an hour. Meanwhile, chop cabbage, divide flower of cauliflower into sprigs, and chop parsley. Add to soup at the end of half an hour with remainder of peas. Cover and simmer till meat and vegetables are tender. Season soup to taste with salt and pepper. Serve in a hot tureen.

When I was a child in Angus, the mutton was kept hot in the oven while we supped the soup. It was served as the meat course with boiled or mashed potatoes and a green vegetable. E.C.

It is said that Queen Victoria was not fond of soup, but her name is more associated with soup than is the name of any other member of the Royal family. In Scotland, a chicken broth bearing the name of 'Victoria' is popular at family parties. When Highland hostesses entertain, Queen Victoria's Cream of Chicken often heads the menu at luncheon or dinner.

LORD WILLIS'S WHITE SOUP *c.* 1869

Bring a knuckle of veal and three pounds of mutton, or an old fowl with three pounds of mutton and five quarts of water to the boil. Add two spoonfuls of rice, one onion with three or four cloves stuck in it, a blade or two of mace, and a few peppercorns. Cover and boil very gently for three hours, then strain and add two ounces of vermicelli and a head of young celery, cut small, to the stock. Boil for one quarter of an hour, stirring all the while. Cut a handful of spinach not too finely. Add to soup. Boil it up fast, then stir in six spoonfuls of cream. Toast a piece of bread and butter it. Put it in broth and serve it up.

PRINCE'S SOUP *c.* 1870

Melt one ounce of butter in a saucepan. Wipe and cut up three pounds of stewing veal and half a pound of lean ham. Wash, dry and joint a calf's foot. Place the veal, ham and foot in saucepan with one or two trimmings of game or poultry, or the carcase of a game bird or chicken. (If using a carcase, break it up before adding.) Scrape and add five Jerusalem artichokes. Slice in two trimmed leeks, two scraped carrots, two peeled turnips and a head of trimmed celery. Add a *bouquet garni*, and half a pint of white stock. Cook over the stove until a thick white glaze forms in bottom of pan, then add two and a half quarts of chicken or veal stock. Bring to boil. Skim, then simmer very gently for one hour. Add one washed anchovy, and one large peeled and cored apple, cut in slices. Simmer gently for one and a half hours. Strain and clarify. Cut four long narrow fillets off the breast of a braised fowl. Spread a layer of chicken forcemeat over each fillet, then brush with beaten egg white. Arrange fillets side by side in a shallow saucepan. Barely cover them with chicken stock. Cover and simmer gently for ten minutes. Melt one ounce of butter in a shallow saucepan, then prepare and thinly slice two sets of lambs' brains and add. Cook over moderate heat until firm, then remove and leave until cold. Beat three eggs with half a cup of chicken stock. Season with salt and pepper to taste. Add half a teaspoon of minced parsley. Pour a layer of the egg mixture, half inch thick, in a flat mould. Steam for three minutes. Cover with a layer of the brains, then with remainder of the custard. Steam for half an hour. Remove mould. When custard is cool, turn out and cut both custard and fillets of fowl into diamond-shaped pieces. Place in a soup tureen. Add boiled asparagus tips. Stir one teaspoon of castor sugar into the soup. Pour it over the garnish.

CARROT SOUP *c.* 1809

Clean and fry four large carrots and two turnips, peeled and cut in slices, till a light brown. Put them into two quarts of strong gravy soup and stew till perfectly tender, then rub them through a sieve. Stir purée into stock. Mix well. Season with salt and pepper to taste. (Add more carrots if you want the soup to be a deep colour.)

EEL SOUP *c.* 1889

Use the head and tail of a large eel, three quarts of water, quarter pound of butter, one leek, the blossoms and leaves of five marigolds, half a pint of green peas or asparagus tips, half a teacup of parsley, a bunch of thyme, two tablespoons of flour, one pint of milk, and salt and pepper to taste. Put the head and tail in a stewpan with the water, and allow to simmer gently for two and a half hours or more till the fish breaks in pieces when tried with a fork. Strain through a china colander. Pour the liquor back into the stewpan. Add butter, and when boiling, throw in prepared leek, green peas (or asparagus), parsley, thyme and marigold leaves, all cut up except the bunch of thyme which should be enclosed in a muslin bag. Cover and simmer till vegetables are tender. Remove muslin bag. Cream flour with a little of the cold milk, then bring remainder of milk to boiling point with marigold blossoms. Strain, then gradually stir hot milk into the creamed flour.

Stir slowly and carefully into the soup to prevent flour
lumping. Keep on stirring after the soup comes to the boil
for about five minutes to remove the rawness from the flour.
(Some cooks prefer not to add the parsley till after the soup
has come to the boil.) Season with pepper and salt. Arrange
slices of toasted bread in the bottom of a tureen. Pour in
soup.

PRINCESS SOUP *c.* 1876

1 roasted boiling fowl
¾ pint boiling veal stock
4 large cucumbers
¼ lb butter
½ lb lean ham
2 sliced onions
2 sprigs of basil
2 bay leaves
1 pint chicken stock
4 tablespoons sago
4 tablespoons flour
1 quart boiling milk
Salt to taste
1 teaspoon sugar
½ pint boiled green peas
1 cup thick cream
Boiled asparagus tips to taste

When the fowl is cold, remove the meat from bones and chop
meat. Pound in a mortar with a pestle. Place bones and
trimmings in a saucepan with the stock. Bring again to boil.
Simmer for half an hour. Peel and thinly-slice cucumbers.
Melt butter in a shallow saucepan. Add ham, onions, basil,
bay leaves and the cucumber slices. Fry quickly for three or
four minutes, stirring occasionally, then add chicken stock.
Simmer for half an hour. Gradually stir in the fowl paste, then
sago. Dilute the flour to a cream with additional cold chicken
stock and stir into soup. When boiling, strain in the stock
from the chicken bones. Simmer gently for 20 minutes. Rub

through a fine hair sieve into another saucepan. Stir until
boiling, then stir in the milk. Bring again to boil, then skim.
Add salt, sugar, and green peas. (If the soup is rather thick,
thin with boiling milk or stock.) Gradually stir in cream.
When hot, but not boiling, place boiled asparagus tips in a
heated soup tureen. Pour in soup gradually, stirring constantly.

WINDSOR SOUP c. 1870

3 calf's feet
2 quarts beef or veal stock
1 quart water
1 *bouquet garni*
½ wineglass Madeira
1 dessertspoon salt
Dash of cayenne pepper
12 *quenelles* of crayfish

Scrape and split feet. Place in a saucepan. Add stock and
water. Bring to simmering point. Skim. Simmer gently, uncovered, until feet are tender, then bone. Cut meat in small
pieces. Strain stock. Measure three pints of the stock into a
saucepan. Add meat from feet, *bouquet garni*, Madeira, salt
and cayenne pepper. Bring again to the boil. Skim if necessary. Simmer for ten minutes. Strain either through a jelly
bag or a fine sieve. Reheat. Add a drop or two of browning
to darken the soup, and crayfish *quenelles* for garnish. Serve
at once.

¶ ALEXANDRA CONSOMMÉ: *Consommé* made from chicken
stock slightly thickened with tapioca and garnished with
shredded lettuce, chervil, *julienne* of chicken breast and tiny
quenelles of chicken.

¶ BALMORAL CREAM SOUP: Cream soup made of calf's
feet stock, flavoured turtle herb, thickened with egg yolk and
cream, and garnished with *julienne* of calf's feet.

¶ Duke of York Consommé: *Consommé* made from game stock, flavoured Marsala, and garnished with small *quenelles* of game and truffle and *julienne* of game. Sometimes it is also garnished with custard dice.

¶ Prince of Wales Consommé: Chicken *consommé*, garnished asparagus tips, custard dice and *quenelles* of chicken and truffle.

¶ Prince of Wales Cream Soup: Cream of veal and calf's head, garnished veal *quenelles*.

¶ Regency Cream Soup: Cream of chicken and barley, garnished with chicken and crayfish *quenelles*, pearl barley and sliced cock's kidneys.

¶ Windsor Cream Soup: Light mock turtle soup, made with calf's feet and garnished *quenelles*.

ROYAL STOCK

(*As made in the royal kitchens today*)

The original of this recipe belonged to Queen Mary's mother, the Duchess of Teck, who was a noted cook and housekeeper.

ROYAL STOCK *c.* 1870

> 4 lbs lean shin of beef
> 4 quarts of spring water
> 1 teaspoonful salt
> 1 carrot
> 1 turnip
> Half a bunch of celery

Cut the meat off the bone into small pieces. Break the bones and remove the marrow. Put meat, bones and water into a stock pot. Add the salt and remove the scum when it arises. When stock is well-skimmed and boiling add the vegetables,

well-washed, peeled or scraped as necessary, and cut into
small pieces. Avoid spices and herbs, and use as little salt as
possible, and no pepper. Thus the stock can be used for any
soup or other dish. Boil slowly for five hours, then strain
through a hair sieve and allow to cool.

*White stock can be prepared in the same way, only it should be made
from veal, poultry or other white meat. E.C.*

FISHERMAN'S SOUP *c.* 1882

The favourite Soup of Princess Louise, Duchess of Argyll

Take one pound each of several freshwater fish of different
kinds, one tomato, two carrots, one leek, two small onions,
a bunch of sweet herbs, one teaspoonful of chilli vinegar, one
teaspoonful soy, enough water to cover the fish, two small
turnips, one head of celery, and pepper and salt to taste.
Wash fish in salt and water. Put them in a stewpan with
tomato, scraped carrots, sliced leek, and peeled and sliced
onions, all lightly fried beforehand. Add a bunch of sweet
herbs. Then put as much water to them as will cover them
and let them stew till contents of pan are reduced to a pulp,
which should be in about three-quarters of an hour. Strain off
the liquor and let it boil another hour. Have ready the turnips,
peeled and cut into cubes, and the celery, washed, scraped and
cut into inch lengths, and both boiled till tender. Add to fish
soup with the chilli vinegar, soy and pepper and salt to taste.

*Just use mixture of fish in the day's catch—carp, dace, roach,
perch, pike, tench, trout, etc. E.C.*

FISH

I CAN find very little sign of any great interest being taken in fish in general by any member of the Royal family except by George the Fifth, who was not only keenly interested in his own oyster beds in the Duchy of Cornwall, but in the whole of the fishing industry. Most of the members of the Royal family are fond of shrimps, specially shrimps caught in Morecambe Bay. When I was in Morecambe, I was told that a supply of shrimps was despatched regularly every week from Morecambe to George the Fifth's table.

The Duke of Windsor, I am told, prefers sole to any other fish. His great-aunt, Princess Louise, Duchess of Argyll, shared not only this taste, but liked fish either in the form of soup or as a course at lunch or dinner.

COD SOUNDS c. 1856

Boil some cod sounds in salted water till tender, then turn on to a dish and stand till cold. Make a forcemeat of chopped oysters, breadcrumbs, butter, yolks of eggs, and seasoning of pepper, salt and grated nutmeg. Fill sounds with the force-meat, roll them up, and skewer them. Lard down each side of each roll with pork or bacon, dredge them with flour, and

B

put them in a tin along with a lump of butter and cook them in a Dutch oven before the fire. Baste with butter till nicely brown, and serve with oyster sauce poured over.

LAMPREYS

In mediæval days, the lamprey, a species of eel, also called 'Nine Eyes' on account of having besides its eyes seven little holes in its head, was a delicacy greatly beloved by royalty. It could be caught from autumn to spring in most tidal rivers, but, like salmon, it has suffered at the hands of industry.

A DISH OF LAMPREYS *c.* 1750

Clean and wash lampreys, removing the black cartilage, and roll them up and place in a stewpan along with prepared shrimps, and two or three chopped anchovies. Season all well with pepper, salt and spices to taste, and cook very slowly with the lid on over a very slow fire in good ale or red wine.

GRILLED LAMPREY *c.* 1766

Scald lamprey, oil the bars of your grid iron with melted butter, and grill him well. Then grind pepper, ginger, cloves and saffron and season fish well, then shake a little pepper inside and serve.

STEWED LAMPREYS *c.* 1745

Clean and wash lampreys carefully and remove the cartilage which runs down the back. Put into a stewpan rolled up like eels, and season with salt and pepper and grated nutmeg. (If more spice is wanted, add ground cloves, mace and allspice to taste.) Cover with equal quantities of strong beef gravy and Madeira or sherry, or with equal quantities of rough cyder, port wine and water. If liked, add an onion, and in that case stick it with four whole cloves and leave out the ground cloves. Stew till tender, covered closely, and if liquor boils too much away, add fresh liquor in a small quantity, but in proportions stated. Remove lampreys to a hot dish when tender. (They will take twice as much time to stew as an ordinary eel.) Melt two ounces of butter in a saucepan. Stir in two ounces of flour, and when it froths, add some of the strained liquid, enough to make a good quantity of gravy. Add two chopped anchovies and boil up. Add lemon juice to taste and made mustard, and serve with sippets of bread. If there is any spawn, fry it in butter and garnish the stew with the bread and spawn alternately. The sauce should take up about a pint of the stock. If more is wanted, you will have to prepare more butter and flour accordingly.

A FINE WAY OF DRESSING SOALES
c. 1680

Take a large pair of soales caught at Dover. Skin them on both sides. Melt some butter in a shallow stew pan. Lay the soles in pan side by side. Add three tablespoonfuls of claret and a dash of anchovy essence. Cover closely. Stew gently till ready. Serve them to table with slyces of lemon or orange.

A DISH OF HERRINGS c. 1860

This recipe is for thirty herring. Clean, wash, split and remove bones from herring, then wash fish in cold water. Sprinkle insides with pepper and salt and roll, and lay in an earthen baking dish. Sprinkle rolls with pepper and salt. Arrange two peeled, sliced onions among the fish, also six cloves, four peppercorns, two blades of mace, and a lump of sugar. Pour over a quart of claret and half a quart of vinegar. Bake in a moderate oven, with a buttered paper over, till fish is tender. Remove paper for five minutes before taking dish out of oven.

LOBSTER BALLS c. 1848

Take a fine hen lobster, two eggs, breadcrumbs, two ounces of butter, pepper, salt and cayenne pepper. Remove the meat from the lobster and pound it in a mortar with the coral and spawn. Mix with it not quite an equal quantity of breadcrumbs seasoned with pepper and salt, and cayenne pepper to taste. Warm the butter and stir into the crumbs and lobster till well mixed. Flour your hands and roll mixture into balls the size of a duck's egg. Brush them over with beaten egg. Coat with breadcrumbs and fry till crisp and golden. Drain on paper and serve very hot.

THE QUEEN MOTHER'S
FILLETS OF SOLE 1928

Take a small whiting and pound it in a mortar with three-pennyworth of lobster coral. [I would just beat in lobster coral to taste.] When well pounded, add one egg white and plenty of seasoning. Beat until blended. Pass through a hair sieve. Place it in a stew pan on ice. When thoroughly chilled, gradually add three-quarters of a pint of cream, half whipped, and test this consistency in boiling water. In the meantime, skin fillets and coat with egg and crumb, then deep-fry. Shape the forcemeat into *quenelles* and poach them in hot water. Serve fillets with cardinal sauce and garnished *quenelles*.

THE MEAT COURSE

Our Second Charles of fame facete
On loin of beef did dine.
He held his sword, pleased, o'er the meat:
'Arise, the famed Sir Loin'.

LONG before the reign of Charles the Second, English beef
was popular at royal tables. In the ancient days, a baron of
beef which consists of both sides of the back, and is really a
double sirloin, sometimes weighing as much as 100 lbs, held
pride of place at many a royal feast. The loin has King Charles
to thank for its title, so legend says. Presented one day with
a fine 'cut off the joint', the famous monarch asked the name
of the joint. When he was told, he drew his sword, smilingly
held it over the joint and said 'For its merit, then I knight it,
and henceforth it shall be called Sir Loin.'

In 1870, Urbain Dubois, Chef de Cuisine to their Majesties
the King and Queen of Prussia, said that nowhere but in
England did a sirloin of beef obtain, on the part of the cooks,
that 'foresight and sacrifice necessary to ensure its perfection'.
The favourite 'remove' on the part of the Crown Princess of

Prussia, by the way, was roast beef and Yorkshire pudding, a taste she inherited from her mother, Queen Victoria, with whom this joint was always a favourite.

The other joint which used to appear frequently on royal tables in Britain was a saddle of lamb. You find it included in almost every royal banquet menu in Victorian and Edwardian days. When it did not appear, lamb cutlets usually took its place.

Prince Albert was very fond of fillet of beef, slit and stuffed with purée of *foie gras*, then larded and braised with Madeira. It was served with *croustades* (hollowed *croutes* of bread or pastry), stuffed with truffles, and the gravy was thickened and flavoured with port wine.

From early days up to the eighteenth century, badger and bear competed with boar and venison for favour at royal tables. It was not until Georgian days that the present custom of serving only meat from domestic animals and venison became the custom. Frederick, Duke of York and Albany, second son of George the Third, was very partial to liver and bacon.

In mediæval days, there was a strong line drawn between the meat served at royal boards and other tables. To quote one historian writing on this subject, 'Pigge for a lord must be "endored" covered with the yolkes of egges.' Only the common people were fortunate enough in olden days to enjoy the 'crackling' as relished today.

CALF'S HEAD CHEESE *c.* 1870

> 1 calf's head
> 1 tablespoon salt
> Pepper to taste
> 1 tablespoon sweet herbs

Boil a calf's head in enough water to cover it till meat falls off the bones. Lift it out, remove meat from bones, and chop small. Season with salt, pepper and herbs to taste. Mix well, then place meat in a colander lined with a linen cloth. Press with a weight on top and turn out when cold.

FORCEMEAT BALLS *c.* 1865

Mince a piece of lean veal and equal quantity of lean bacon very finely, then add a double quantity of minced beef suet. Beat well in a mortar, and sprinkle with a little water while beating. Season with pepper, salt, cloves and mace, grated lemon peel and crushed sweet herbs to taste. Moisten with beaten yolk of egg, and shape into balls with floured hands. Boil them for two or three minutes, and then fry them in deep boiling hot lard or dripping.

FRIED LAMB CUTLETS *c.* 1880

6 lamb cutlets
Salt and pepper to taste
1½ ozs butter
1 teaspoon meat glaze
1 tablespoon white wine
1 teaspoon lemon juice
½ teaspoon chopped chervil or tarragon

Trim cutlets neatly and season on both sides with salt and pepper. Melt butter in a frying pan and fry cutlets lightly on both sides. When ready, serve in a circle or oval on a hot dish. Strain off butter. Add glaze and wine, lemon juice, herbs and a large pat of extra butter. Heat and pour over cutlets. Enough for three persons.

POTTED BEEF *c.* 1868

Cut six lbs of lean beef in slices, then pound a quarter of an ounce of saltpetre, half an ounce of prunella, and one and a half ounces of common salt together, then rub mixture well over the beef. Put beef in a deep pan, and turn it every day for three days, then pour a pint of water, and the brine in pan into a roasting tin. Place beef in tin, and bake for three hours in a moderate oven, when remove from liquor, drain well and pick away all skin. Shred well. Chop and pound in a stone mortar, adding seasoning to taste of black pepper, nutmeg and ground mace. Add enough melted butter to the meat to enable you to beat it to the consistency of paste. Squeeze into pots. Pour a little clarified butter over each and cover like jam.

You can pot hare and venison in the same way. Only omit salt-petre and use a little more common salt to make up for it. E.C.

HUNTER'S BEEF *c.* 1856

Round of beef
1 grated nutmeg
1 oz black peppercorns
¼ oz allspice berries
2 ozs powdered saltpetre
1 oz whole cloves
¼ lb granulated sugar
2 handfuls of salt

Hang beef for three days, then bone. Pound remainder of ingredients to the finest powder. Place the beef in a crock. Rub spices, etc into the meat. Turn it once a day for three weeks, then wash meat in cold water, and bind it into shape with tape. Place in a saucepan. Add half a pint of cold water. Sprinkle top of the meat with shredded suet, then cover pan closely with a paste made of flour and water. Bake in a slow oven for six hours. Remove and leave until cold. Remove paste and tape. Glaze and garnish with chopped aspic jelly.

KING GEORGE THE FIFTH'S MUTTON CUTLETS *c.* 1930

This recipe, which is treasured by every royal cook, was given to me by a Lady-in-Waiting who says that King George's aunt always had mutton cutlets cooked for him in this way when the King chose to lunch or dine with her. He had a very delicate digestion in his later years. Indeed, so delicate was the King's digestion that before he went any-where on a visit a list of the foods he was allowed to eat was sent in advance on the advice of his physicians. Mutton cutlets is said to be the only fried dish his doctors would permit him to have.

Prepare cutlets by trimming them and dipping each one in a mixture of yolk of raw eggs and toasted breadcrumbs. Turn each several times in the batter, then have a quantity of the finest mutton fat melting in a deep frying pan. When so hot that a little vapour arises or a piece of bread thrown into it immediately turns golden brown, place cutlets gently at once into the boiling fat and cook for two and a half minutes on one side, when they should be golden brown, so turn. Cook for two and a half minutes on other side. Remove, drain carefully on absorbent paper, and serve very hot. Be careful neither to undercook nor overcook or they will be indigestible.

MUTTON CUTLETS FAVOURED BY QUEEN VICTORIA *c.* 1860

6 ozs cold roast mutton
3 ozs sieved breadcrumbs
1 saltspoon salt
Coralline pepper to taste
2 ozs minced mushrooms
1 oz truffles
½ teaspoon curry powder
1½ ozs butter
1½ ozs flour
½ pint rich beef stock

Weigh the mutton without skin or bone. Mince finely. Place in a basin. Add crumbs, salt, coralline pepper and mushrooms. Dice truffles and add. Stir in curry powder. Melt butter in a small shallow saucepan. Add flour. When blended, stir in stock. Stir till smooth and boiling, then add the mixed ingredients. Stir till blended. Turn on to a buttered plate. Chill. Divide in eight equal portions. Shape into cutlets. Egg and crumb. Fry in hot fat until golden brown—about five minutes. Slip a stalk of macaroni one and a half inches long, into each. Dish up in a circle. Fill centre with fried parsley sprigs.

B*

LORD CLIVE'S CURRY *c.* 1750

6 sliced onions
2 green apples
1 clove of garlic
1 clove
Juice and grated rind of $\frac{1}{2}$ lemon
A little stock
1 teaspoon good curry powder
Salt to taste
Walnut of butter
1 teaspoon flour

Stew sliced onions with apples, garlic, clove, lemon rind and stock for five minutes, then add curry powder, lemon juice and about half a teaspoonful of salt. Roll butter in flour and add. Stir till boiling. You can cook in this curry any kind of raw meat cut up into small pieces, or can heat up pieces of cooked meat in the sauce when it is ready to serve.

ROASTED NEAT'S TONGUE *c.* 1778

OX'S OR COW'S TONGUE

Boil a pickled tongue until the skin comes loose. Remove skin. Stick tongue with cloves, about two inches asunder. Wrap a veal caul round it and roast it for half an hour in a fairly quick oven. [In olden days, it was prepared in the same way and roasted on a spit.] Remove the caul. Dish up. Garnish it with sieved raspings of bread and slices of lemon. Serve with gravy or claret sauce.

TO IMPROVE THE FLAVOUR OF A HAM
c. 1800

Soak for twelve hours, fleshy part downwards. Drain, sew tightly in muslin, then place in pan. Cover with cold water. Bring slowly to the boil. Simmer till half ready. Drain off water. Add four quarts of Champagne, Claret, or vinegar, and fresh cold water to cover. Bring again to boil. Cook very slowly till tender.

SCOTCH COLLOPS

In olden days, Scotch collops were made of veal, and sometimes called 'White Collops'. They were often served with oysters and mushrooms. Nowadays, stewing steak is more generally used. I am giving you an old-fashioned recipe for Scotch collops and a modern one which in Scotland, is usually called 'mince', or 'mince collops'.

OLD FASHIONED SCOTCH COLLOPS
1789

Cut very thin slices from gammon of bacon. Brown a little butter in a stewpan, being careful not to burn it. Fry gammon thoroughly, then take it out and keep hot while you fry lightly some slices of veal. Dish up the veal. Add a little boiling water to the gravy, also a finely-minced onion, a dash of nutmeg, and pepper to taste. Boil a few minutes. Heat up gammon in it, then remove gammon. Strain gravy. Thicken with a little flour and heat up. Add a cup of fried mushrooms, the strained juice of a lemon and some fried or baked forcemeat balls. Pour over the veal. Garnish with gammon.

SCOTCH OR MINCE COLLOPS (MINCE)
1848

1 oz butter or dripping
1 lb minced stewing steak
1 peeled onion
Salt and pepper to taste
1 cup water

Melt butter or dripping in a shallow saucepan. Add steak. Stir with a wooden spoon over slow heat till all the meat turns brown. Slice and chop onion and add to meat. Season with salt and pepper to taste. Add water. Cover. Simmer gently from thirty-five to forty minutes, stirring occasionally. If liked thickened, either add a dessertspoonful of oatmeal or of breadcrumbs to the meat after the water, or thicken with cornflour or flour creamed with cold water just before dishing up. In some parts of Scotland, this dish is left unthickened, and oatmeal puddings are pricked and added to it (allowing four to a pound of steak) about fifteen minutes before dishing up. In other parts of Scotland, it is crowned with poached eggs, allowing one to each person. To serve mince, pile on a hot ashet [meat platter]. Garnish round the base with sippets of toast.

SHEEP TROTTERS' JELLY *c.* 1799

Put six quarts of water and four sheep's feet into a saucepan. Boil until reduced to one quart, then add two quarts of water. Boil until reduced to one quart. Pour into a basin. Cover and stand overnight. Skim off fat. Add a quart of new milk with an ounce of cinnamon, and a little sugar to taste. Boil for twenty minutes, stirring constantly, then remove from heat. Pour into a basin. Stir until cold.

TO MAKE SAUSAGES *c.* 1887

Take one pound of lean veal, one pound of lean pork, one and a half pounds of beef suet, and one handful of sage. Chop altogether very small and season with pepper and salt and nutmeg, then beat meat in a mortar. Add four yolks of eggs. Roll pieces up in the form of sausages. Rub frying pan with a walnut of butter, and fry them when pan is hot, keeping them moving gently about to prevent them sticking.

GAME AND POULTRY

In Mediæval days there were few birds in Britain that did not find their way to the Court table in some form or another. Blackbirds, bitterns, cranes, herons, larks, ortolans, snipe, sparrows, spoonbills, thrushes and wheatears were as popular as capons, ducks and geese.

Sometimes larks and ortolans were made into a pudding or pie with veal and ham. Sometimes they were roasted on a lark-spit before a bright fire. All the roasting was done on spits in those days, when fat capons hung cheek by jowl with sucking pigs, woodcocks and other birds fit 'to set before the King'. Woodcock has always been popular at Court, sharing favour with the partridge.

> *If partridge had the woodcock's thighs,*
> *'Twould be noblest bird that flies;*
> *If woodcock had the partridge breast,*
> *'Twould be the best bird ever drest.*

Woodcock is usually served roasted like partridge or grouse in Britain, but the connoisseur prefers it *flambée*. Lightly roasted and carved, it is placed in a casserole or timbale with a little freshly-ground white pepper. A glass of brandy is next poured over and set alight, then the juice of the carcase is pressed out, mixed with thickened gravy and poured over portions before serving.

Henry the Eighth had a fancy for bitterns. This rare bird, known as 'the bull bird' because of its booming call, was regularly served at his Court.

Michaelmas goose, I am told, is an annual guest at Royal tables. It is said that Queen Elizabeth the First was eating roast goose on Michaelmas Day when the news was conveyed to her that the Armada was routed, so she issued a command that roast goose should be the national fête dish for Michaelmas Day from that time onwards.

Queen Victoria was very fond of game, particularly pheasant and woodcock, cooked in the following way: add chopped truffle and *foie gras* to taste to a good herb stuffing. Stuff, truss and place bird in a casserole with a little Madeira wine. Cover and braise. Thicken gravy to taste and add a little chopped truffle before serving.

All through the ages, pigeons have been considered a delicacy, not only at the Royal table, but at the tables of the nobles. In the sumptuous days, every large establishment had its dove cote, which was robbed for the table. In the eighteenth century, pigeons were jugged and stuffed and stewed, and made into elaborate pies. Nowadays they are usually stewed.

It was not until 1540 that turkeys were introduced to the Royal table. Some say they came from Asia, some from Africa. Others assert they flew over from Turkey! Vasco da Gama also gets the credit of importing them from Mexico in the middle of the sixteenth century. Brillat Savarin, the famous writer on culinary matters, insists that the bird is of trans-Atlantic origin. No matter where the turkey came from, it soon put the nose of the swan out of joint, not to mention those of the bustard and the peacock, at Royal banquets. In Tudor days, turkeys were very expensive. Mary of England and Philip of Spain were very fond of turkey chicks cooked on the spit.

Henry the Fourth, George the Fourth and Queen Alexandra all seemed to prefer chicken. One of George the Fourth's favourite dishes was a boiled fowl, masked Allemande sauce and garnished with crayfish butter and cox-combs. Queen Alexandra preferred a fricassée of chicken garnished with asparagus tips. Edward the Seventh liked a plump capon stuffed with rice, *foie gras* and truffle, and braised with rich stock. It was usually garnished with asparagus tips and served with creamed cucumber and sauce suprême, flavoured with curry. When he was Prince of Wales, a very elaborate capon dish was named after him. The bird was stuffed with *foie gras* and minced woodcock, then braised and served garnished with cooked mushrooms, truffles and fillets of woodcock, in thickened gravy.

The Duke of Connaught was said to prefer pheasant to any other bird. One of his favourite recipes, I am told, was pheasant stuffed with chestnuts and roasted, then simply served on a *croute* of toast with thickened gravy. It only had a watercress salad for company.

CHEKYNS IN SAUCE 1580

Taken from an old cookery book belonging to the Princess

To dight chekyns in sauce, tak a whole chekyn—if for commons chopped, if for a lord use the whole chekyns—and boil in sweet broth of beef [good stock] with a quantity of wyne, and when the chekyn be cooked enough tak out of ye pot and bette the yolks of many egges hard-boiled in a mortar with sage to taste, and parsley, and along with good wyne. Drain throughe a fine hair sieve and put thereto poudre of cloves, sugar, canelles and a little veniger, and salt to taste. Colour it with saffron. Then couche the chekyn in a hot dish and put the syrup in dyshes an serve it with the chekyn.

A SUPPER DISH 210 YEARS OLD
c. 1778

Half-boil cockscombs, as many as you will. Open them with care, using the point of a knife. Take the white flesh of fowl, as much bacon and beef marrow, and cut these meats small, then beat very fine on a marble slab in a mortar with a pestle. Season them with pepper, salt and grated nutmeg, and mix with yolks of eggs and fill the cockscombs with the mixture. Stew in a little excellent meat juice or gravy for half an hour along with some freshly gathered mushrooms and half as many pickled mushrooms. Beat up the yolks of one or two eggs. Add to the gravy, stirring it constantly till thickened. Season with salt then dish on a hot platter.

This was a favourite dish of Queen Victoria's mother, the Duchess of Kent. E.C.

TO COOK HARE *c.* 1835

'Receipt given by my Uncle, the King, William IV.' VICTORIA, *January* 1835

Dight carefully a hare, preparing it for cooking and taking care that none of the blood, liver or giblets are lost. Cut into pieces and dry without washing first upon a cloth. Then roast some slices of onion in a gill of boiling fat, and throw them with the meat of the hare into a large earthenware pot. Add thereto seasoning of herbs, garlic, though of that but little, onions, chillies, salt, pepper and a very small 'trifle' of mace. Then into this mixture cast some slices of bacon and pour upon the whole sufficient red wine and rich stock—in equal proportions—to moisten. Set the pot over the fire, and bring the contents slowly to boiling heat. Skim and stir frequently, then leave to simmer slowly till the meat be very tender. Thirty minutes before it is finished cooking, add to the stew the liver, giblets and blood. When ready, place the whole in a hot bowl or dish—silver or pewter are the dishes advised as they retain heat for a long while—and serve at once.

QUAILS A LA PRINCESS LOUISE *c.* 1895

Allowing one quail for each person, bone and stuff with the following mixture: Put a quarter pound of raw chicken meat in a mortar with a tablespoon of cold Béchamel sauce, and two egg whites. Pound well, then rub through a wire sieve.

Add freshly-ground white pepper and salt to taste to the purée, then stir in a quarter pint very thick cream and one or two chopped truffles. Stuff each bird and sew up with fine white twine. Poach in white stock for eight minutes. Leave the birds until quite cold. Carefully remove the string then spread all over with a thin layer of *foie gras*. Coat with *chaud-froid* sauce. Decorate with ornaments of truffle, then mask with liquefied aspic jelly. Arrange birds in a circle around serving dish. Fill the circle with *macedoine* of spring vegetables, preparing equal quantity of cooked asparagus tips, carrots, green peas, potatoes and turnips, all cut in pea shapes. They should be boiled separately, then drained thoroughly on a napkin. Mix a pint of the *macedoine* with a pint of diced pineapple. Place them in a *bombe* mould. Fill mould with strained liquefied aspic jelly. Leave until set. Turn out into the centre of the birds. Decorate round the birds with a piping of aspic jelly.

PISH PASH *c.* 1883

A huge boiling fowl
A blade of mace
Pepper and salt
½ cupful of rice

Cut fowl in two. Put half the fowl into spring water, about a quart. Boil till the meat is in rags, then strain off the meat and to the liquor add the other half fowl, cut up into joints, mace, pepper and salt. Stew gently till joints are half cooked. Add rice and cook till very tender and nearly all the gravy is absorbed, when remove the blade of mace and serve.

SOUFFLE OF CHICKEN *c.* 1899

As cooked for Princess Louise, Duchess of Argyll

Strip from the bones the whole meat of a chicken and pass it twice through a mincing machine, then pound in a mortar. Now rub through a sieve in order to separate all gristle and

fibres. Add two or three beaten eggs, and three tablespoons
of fresh thick cream. Mix well together. Season well with
pepper and salt, and pour gently into a buttered mould.
Steam for twenty minutes.

STEW OF PIGEONS *c.* 1848

Take pigeons and beat them flat. Put butter in a stewpan.
Brown it very well, and put pigeons therein, and fry them till
brown. Cover with beef juice or gravy. Add a bunch of sweet
herbs, an onion, and white wine with some flour for thickening. Allow stew to cook slowly till thick, then squeeze in
juice of a large lemon and garnish with herbs.

STEWED STUFFED PIGEONS *c.* 1839

Make some forcemeat balls, one for each bird required, of
grated breadcrumbs, beef suet, sprinkled with flour and
shredded, a little chopped bacon and thyme, grated lemon
peel, marjoram and parsley to taste. Moisten with a little
melted butter and the yolks of two eggs and shape into balls.
Put one in each bird. Tie birds up closely, and fry in butter
till almost brown enough, when stew a little while in made
gravy and white wine, thickening gravy before serving with
butter and flour, and sharpening with lemon juice.

'MY UNCLE'S FAVOURITE RECEIPT FOR COOKING VENISON' *c.* 1843

Taken from an old notebook

Wash a haunch of venison with fresh milk and water and dry
it vigorously with a clean linen towel. Then powder it with
dry ginger in order to keep the fly away and afterwards
'hang' for a time. Some prefer that the venison shall be kept
for a long period, others for a shorter. It should be carefully
watched and when it is ready to be used, should be washed in
warm water before cooking.

To Roast as Receipt Directs: A haunch will require about

three and a half hours to roast. Wash it just before setting to roast in vinegar and water and dry well, then cover with buttered paper, and baste with fresh butter till nearly cooked. Then boil a pint of good claret with nutmeg, cloves, mace and pepper. Strain and pour over venison and serve with sweet sauce.

ROYAL VENISON *c.* 1836

Scrape off coating of flour, and wrap in an envelope or coffyn [casing] of suet dough. Cover all with oiled paper, tied on with strings, and place joint before a regular red fire—very fierce. When cooked, put off envelope and season with salt, sprinkle with a few particles of flour, and a large quantity of melted fresh butter, and brown as quickly as possible. Large joints of venison must be served highly flavoured.

VENISON STEAKS *c.* 1859

Choose tender steaks cut from loin, from half to three-quarters inch thick, to taste. Brush them freely with olive oil, flavoured with lemon juice or vinegar, and a pinch of crushed herbs. Stand for half an hour, then turn and stand for another half hour. Drain. Season with salt and pepper. Grill from ten to fifteen minutes, according to thickness and whether liked rare or well-done. Serve each crowned with a slowly-fried mushroom stuffed with a pat of *maitre d'hôtel* butter, and with red currant jelly.

VEGETABLES

'IF THE vegetables to be koocked be for common folk they should be thickked with grated bred, if for a lord yolkes of eggs should be used.'

A DISH OF PEAS *c.* 1856

Boil two pounds shelled peas till tender, in salted boiling water, then drain thoroughly. Now place in a stewpan, add a heaped teaspoon of butter, toss them lightly in this for three minutes, then add a shaking of powdered sugar, a good dust of ground cinnamon, and just enough thick cream to make peas creamy. Make piping hot and serve by themselves.

BAKED POTATOES AU PARMESAN *c.* 1884

Scrub till quite clean as many potatoes of a large even size as you think you will need. Dry them and bake them in their jackets in a moderate oven till soft to the touch. Remove from oven, cut in halves, lengthwise, and scoop out insides, taking care not to break the skins when doing so. Mash potato with a fork, then beat with a wooden spoon till light, adding butter, a little cream, grated Parmesan cheese and pepper and salt to taste. Put mixture back in potato cases, score with the prongs of a fork, sprinkle with a little grated Parmesan and brown under the grill.

This method of cooking potatoes was said to be popular with the Prince of Wales. E.C.

ENDIVE *c.* 1879

4 or 5 heads of endive
A large piece of butter
A little salt
2 dessertspoons white sauce
¾ wineglassful of cream
2 lumps of sugar

Wash the endive, remove roots, and pick off outer leaves, preserving only the white portions. Put these in a saucepan of boiling salted water. Boil quickly without the lid, till tender. Drain well in a colander. Squeeze dry, chop finely and rub through a coarse hair sieve into a stewpan. Add the butter and salt. Stir over a slow fire for a few moments before mixing in the white sauce and cream and sugar. Stir purée over fire till thick enough to pile up in a hot vegetable dish. Garnish with sippets of toast.

SALSIFY *c.* 1845

This is delicious served with broiled steaks. Wash and scrape one bunch salsify and put at once into cold water to which you have also added the juice of a lemon. Allow it to stand for ten minutes. Then cut crosswise in one inch slices, and cook covered, in boiling salted water. Drain it when soft. Add three tablespoons of butter, and sprinkle with one teaspoon chopped parsley, half a teaspoon of minced chives, and salt and pepper to taste.

SORREL *c.* 1783

Mary Queen of Scots, it is said, introduced sorrel to Scotland. I am told that it can be seen growing wild round a little village near Holyrood where her retainers were allowed to settle after their unhappy Queen lost her life.

TO STEW: Wash thoroughly as you would spinach. Place in a silver vessel or a stone jar with only the water that clings to the leaves. Simmer very gently until tender, stirring occasionally so that the sorrel cooks evenly. Add butter to taste and beat well. Serve with roast chicken or veal.

I would cook it in an enamel saucepan. E.C.

TO BOYLE A COLLY-FLOWER *c.* 1739

Wash and trim your colly-flower. Boyle it in plenty of milk and water, but no salt, until it be tender. When ready to dish it up, place boyled greens in a hot dish. Lay colly-flower on top. Cover it with good melted butter.

TO COOK DANDELIONS *c.* 1835

'Dish Good for Health.' VICTORIA, 1835

Wash some dandelions, boil some salt and water and while boiling put therein the dandelions. Cook till tender, take from the fire and hold under running water to prevent dandelions becoming too yellow and bitter. Then put into a pan a piece of butter, add a spoonful of flour and stock. Stir well till smooth and cooked, then add dandelions and season with salt and pepper to taste. Cook for twelve minutes longer, stirring well.

TO STEW SPINAGE *c.* 1736

Wash spinage well in several waters. Place in a cullendar. Have ready a large pan of boyling water with a handful of salt. Put it in, let it boyle two minutes. It will take off the strong earthy taste, then put it into a sieve. Squeeze well. Put a quarter of a pound of butter into a tossing pan. Put in your spinage. Keep turning and chopping it with a knife until it be quite dry and green. Lay it upon a plate. Press it with

another. Cut in the shape of sippets or diamonds. Pour round
it melted butter.

SALLETTS *c.* 1673

In the days of King Charles the Second, a dressing for salad
was described as 'a careful mixture of mustard, oil and
vinegar, with or without hard-boiled egg.' This was mixed in
a bowl of porcelain or of Holland Delft with a wooden or
glass spoon.

A SIMPLE SALLETT *c.* 1793
OF GEORGE THE THIRD'S

Take one green vegetable such as a young lettuce. Mix with
cold boiled carrots, chives and radish roots. Serve plain on a
dish after dressing with fresh olive oil, vinegar and sugar.

A COMPOUND SALLETT *c.* 1793

To the Simple Sallett add a mixture of young buds, and knots
of all manner of wholesome herbs at their first springing,
mixed with red sage, mint, violets, marigolds, spinage, etc.
Blanched almonds, raisins, figs, capers, olives, currants,
oranges and lemon, sliced fish, flesh, and fowl may also be
added to the grand sallett.

¶ HENRY VI SALAD: Dice new potatoes, mix with
smoked sardines and moisten with dressing, flavoured *fines
herbes. c.* 1443.

¶ MARY QUEEN OF SCOTS SALAD: Dice sliced boiled
celeriac and lettuce, moisten with cream, sharpened with
vinegar. Garnish with chopped truffle and chervil and slices
of hard-boiled egg. *c.* 1583.

¶ PRINCE OF WALES' SALAD: Lettuce and watercress,
dressed with French dressing, flavoured minced chervil and
capers. Garnish with fillets of sardines, and diced pimiento, or
strips of pimiento. *c.* 1935.

¶ REGENT'S SALAD: Boiled, diced lamb's tongue, mixed with boiled, diced celeriac, new potatoes and cucumber. Garnish with asparagus tips and lettuce. *c.* 1815.

¶ VICTORIA SALAD: Diced celeriac mixed with diced potatoes and sliced artichoke bottoms. Moistened mayonnaise, coloured pink with beetroot juice. Garnish with asparagus tips and chopped or sliced truffles. *c.* 1854.

¶ WINDSOR SALAD: Diced boiled chicken and tongue, mixed to taste with shredded celery, chopped truffle and piccalilli. Dress with mayonnaise. *c.* 1912.

JUNE BUD SALLETT *c.* 1782

6 lettuce hearts
6 tablespoons diced boiled fowl
6 steamed mushrooms
Salt and pepper to taste
Watercress and rosemary
12 radish roses

Prepare lettuce hearts and carefully remove each centre. Crisp in ice-cold water, then dry. Arrange each equal distance apart round a shallow glass bowl. Mix fowl with mushrooms. Season with salt and pepper, and coat to taste with mayonnaise. Chill. When required, carefully fill hearts. Sprinkle filling with a dust of parsley. Place sprigs of watercress in centre. Decorate it with one or two spikes of flowering rosemary, lavender or mint. Wreath with radish roses.

SAUCES

ONE OF the most famous sauces in the Royal kitchen is Béarnaise. Henry the Fourth, who was a great gourmand, was probably the inspiration of this sauce, as it is named after his birth-place, Béarn. Usually when any entrée is named 'Henry Fourth', such as *Filet de Bœuf* or *Tournedos Henry Fourth*, it is served with Béarnaise Sauce.

¶ FILET DE BŒUF BÉARNAISE: Grilled or fried fillet of beef served on artichoke bottoms, and masked Béarnaise sauce enriched with meat glaze. Garnished with sprigs of watercress, *noisette* potatoes, and olive-shaped potatoes *sautéed* in butter.

BEARNAISE SAUCE *c.* 1402

4 shallots
½ gill malt vinegar
½ gill tarragon vinegar
6 peppercorns
¼ pint Béchamel sauce
4 egg yolks
3 ozs butter

Peel and chop shallots. Place in a saucepan with the vinegars and crushed peppercorns. Bring to boil. Boil till vinegar is reduced to one third of original quantity. Strain on to Béchamel sauce, stirring constantly. Stir till hot, then remove pan to side of stove, and stir in egg yolks, one at a time, with a wooden spoon. Return to stove, and stir over a slow heat till thickened, but do not allow sauce to boil. Add butter, bit by bit, allowing each piece to melt before putting in the next.

One of the most elaborate cold sauces in the Royal kitchen is named 'Prince of Wales'. It is a blend of two well-known sauces called 'Gothic' and 'Vincent'.

¶ To Make Gothic: Pound chillies with hard-boiled eggs. Flavour with saffron and mix to a cream with oil and vinegar. Season to taste with salt and cayenne pepper.

¶ To Make Vincent: Pound hard-boiled eggs with chopped chervil, chives, tarragon, watercress and parsley. Mix with a little blanched pounded sorrel and spinach. Beat in a mortar till smooth, then sieve, and stir in mayonnaise to taste. Flavour with Worcester sauce.

CHEROKEE SAUCE c. 1810

Mix a quart of walnut pickle with a half pint of mushroom catsup, six finely-chopped anchovies, one ounce of cayenne pepper, half an ounce of minced garlick, one ounce of minced shallots, one drachm of cochineal and four spoonfuls of Indian soy. Bottle. Cork tightly and shake well once a day. The longer it is kept before it is served the better.

GRAVY FOR PIES

Rich veal stock with a little butter, ham or bacon, peeled mushrooms, peeled onions, sweet herbs, a little carrot, lemon peel, allspice, cloves and mace. A little brown gravy may be added or cream if a white sauce is wanted. Boil slowly for two hours, then strain. Do not add cream till after sauce is strained and when you heat up sauce take care you do not let it boil or it will curdle.

KING EDWARD THE SEVENTH'S SAUCE

From Queen Victoria's book, dated 1861. Recipe in unknown handwriting. This sauce is known in the Royal kitchens today as 'King Edward the Seventh's Sauce'. It was originally invented for His Royal Highness in the year 1861, long before he ascended the throne.

Take four hard-boiled yolks of eggs, four anchovies, washed and wiped, a handful of tarragon, chervil, burnet, chives— these to be well par-boiled and afterwards pressed in a cloth to extract all water—a tablespoonful of capers, a tablespoonful of French mustard, and three raw yolks of eggs. Place all these in a mortar and bruise together with a pestle, and then proceed to work in nearly half a pint of fresh salad oil and half a gill of tarragon vinegar by degrees. When this is done, rub the sauce produced through a hair sieve. This to be eaten with boiled fish or meats. It also makes a good dressing for fish, game and poultry salads.

PLUM PUDDING SAUCE 1911

½ lb unsalted butter
Pinch of salt
15 ozs sifted icing sugar
Juice of 1 lemon
½ cup brandy
¼ cup port wine
1 egg white
1 cup thick cream

Beat butter to a cream with salt and sugar. Strain and stir in lemon juice by degrees, then beat in brandy and port wine gradually. Beat well, then fold in lightly-whipped white of egg and thickly-whipped cream. Pile in a mound in a glass dish. Dust lightly with grated nutmeg, and cinnamon if liked. Serve at once.

QUEEN MARY FIRST'S SAUCE *c.* 1556

TO SERVE WITH SHOULDER OF MUTTON

Three-parts roast a well-hung shoulder of mutton, then put a soup plate under it with a quarter cup each of hot water and port wine, a shallot, one anchovy, finely chopped, and a little pepper. Baste the meat with this and the gravy that drops from it. When meat is tender place on a hot dish, the inside upwards. Score it with a knife, pour the gravy over, and sprinkle thickly with fine fresh breadcrumbs fried in butter.

REGENT'S PIQUANT SAUCE *c.* 1820

6 shallots
4 cloves
1 blade mace
1 oz cayenne pepper
1 quart vinegar
$\frac{1}{4}$ pint soy
$\frac{1}{4}$ pint mushroom ketchup
1 teaspoon essence of anchovy

Peel and place shallots in a wide-mouthed bottle. Add cloves, mace, cayenne pepper and vinegar. Cork. Infuse for ten days, shaking bottle daily. Strain through a funnel into another bottle. Add soy, mushroom ketchup and anchovy essence. Shake thoroughly, then pour into small bottles. Cork tightly

REGENT'S RUM SAUCE *c.* 1820

1 egg yolk
$\frac{1}{4}$ pint thin cream
$\frac{1}{2}$ tablespoon castor sugar
1 tablespoon rum
Vanilla essence to taste

Beat egg yolk and cream in the top of a double boiler over hot water till blended, and the custard coats the back of a spoon. Stir in sugar. When dissolved, remove from heat and gradually stir in rum, then vanilla. Serve in a hot sauceboat with plum pudding and Regent's Pudding.

SAUCE FOR WILD DUCK *c.* 1710

Take winter savory, thyme and sage, of each a little; put this very small into some strong broth, a little pepper, salt, a little ginger, two spoonfuls of claret, and two spoonfuls of mutton gravy, and boyle all this a quarter of an hour; put in the gravy that drops from the ducks, but none of the fat of them. When the ducks are three-quarters roasted, pour the same through them; and when they are cut up, put them on a chafing dish of coals, and stew them a little.

SAUCE PIQUANT FOR CHICKEN *c.* 1707

Squeeze the juice from an orange, strain it, then add white wine, rose water, ground ginger, ground mace, sugar and melted butter to taste. Cook over the fire till well mixed and mellow then serve.

STRAWBERRY SAUCE *c.* 1515

As made by the cook of King Henry the Eighth

Take of powdered rue, powdered dandelion flowers and roots, pepper and salt. Work them in a mortar with a pestle along with the yolks of hard-boiled egges, and mingle with hot sour milk. Serve with hot strawberries.

This sauce would make a better dressing for boiled or steamed fish, or for a salad made of boiled root vegetables. E.C.

WHITE OYSTER SAUCE *c.* 1852

Wash fifty oysters one by one in a basin of clean water, then run your oyster liquor through a fine strainer. Put oysters in a

pan along with their liquor and half boil them, then remove
them and some of the liquor, and add a pint of cream to
remainder of liquor along with a little mace and a quarter
pound of butter worked up with enough flour to make sauce
proper thickness. Boil up, add oysters, finish cooking and
when ready, remove from fire, and add a glass of white wine
by degrees. When flavoured to taste, set it over the fire again,
stirring till piping hot, but do not boil in case the boiling
'turns' the sauce.

SAUCE A LA REINE *c.* 1831

1 boiling fowl
½ lb lean ham
6 peeled shallots
2 blades of mace
3½ pints rich white stock
2 ozs butter
½ pint cream

Cut up the fowl and the ham. Slice shallots. Place all in a
shallow saucepan with mace and half a pint of the stock.
Bring to boil. Simmer gently for a quarter of an hour, then
stir in remainder of stock. Bring to boil. Boil for half an hour,
then strain it off. Melt butter in a saucepan. Add as much
flour as will dry it up, then stir in the strained stock. When
boiling, draw pan to side and gradually stir in the cream.
Boil for two or three minutes, stirring constantly. Strain
through a tammy cloth and use.

SAUCE TO SERVE WITH BOYLED
MUTTON *c.* 1702

Place a good handful of capers into about a pint of claret wine.
Flavour it to taste with some nutmeg. Cook slowly over
coles for a few minutes, then stir in butter to taste in small
pieces.

PASTRIES, PASTIES
AND PIES

Sing a song of sixpence,
A pocket full of rye
Four and twenty blackbirds
Baked in a pie.

When the pie was opened
The birds began to sing
Wasn't that a dainty dish
To set before a King?

FASHIONS in birds have changed since this old rhyme was composed, but the pie is still as popular as it was in Tudor days. During the reigns of Charles the Second, James the Second, William and Mary, and Queen Anne, pies were seasonal. In the spring, skerret and oyster pies were among those most frequently served. In the summer, humble (venison) pie was most popular at Court. During the winter season, it gave place to artichoke and steak pies.

In the seventeenth century, most unholy mixtures (by present-day standards) were imprisoned in pastry, then baked and served, such as a combination of larks or sparrows and oysters, mixed with chestnuts and dates, sharpened with pickled barberries and moistened with egg.

In the days of Henry the First, it was the custom of the City of Gloucester to send a lamprey pie to the King at Christmas when he held his Court, but although this monarch is said to have died through over-indulgence of this dish, this is no reflection on the City of Gloucester as the tragedy happened at Rouen. It is stated on the tomb of John of Plantagenet that he died of a surfeit of lampreys. It does not seem possible that both expired from the same cause! The death of the King had no effect on the custom, as it would have had in modern times. The City of Gloucester continued to send a lamprey pie to the Court every Christmas until eighteen hundred and thirty-six, when the custom died on account of shortage of funds.

Queen Elizabeth also confessed to a fondness for lamprey pie. In her own words, it was 'one of my passions'. In Queen Victoria's Jubilee Year, a lamprey pie was made in an oval shape. It was baked with a raised crust and garnished with aspic jelly and crayfish and truffles fixed with gold skewers. The pie weighed twenty pounds, and was a most elaborate affair.

The heads of the skewers were in the shape of crowns and the gold crown and sceptre decorated the top, while four gold lions kept guard round the base. Two silk bannerettes waved on either side. One was emblazoned with the Gloucester coat-of-arms, and the other with two lampreys and the words 'Royal Lamprey Pie'. The custom of sending lamprey pies to Court, which began in the days of the Normans, is now discontinued. The last record I can find of a pie being sent to Court was at Christmas nineteen hundred and thirty, when King George the Fifth received a present of 'twenty-four woodcocks "baked in a pie",' from the Governor-General of the Irish Free State. This custom dates back to the time of George the Third when Lord Talbot, who was then Viceroy of Ireland, presented the King with a pie containing twenty-four woodcocks, which were then highly prized in Ireland.

PASTRY

Some Notes and Remarks on the Making of Pastry Which Were Given to me by the Baroness and by Others. VICTORIA

(1) Pastry is best when made upon a marble slab or table.

(2) Cleanliness is essential.

(3) The flour should be of the finest quality.

(4) Pastry should be baked in a 'quick' oven and should be slightly browned.

(5) The butter should be very fresh and slightly salted.

(6) Lard can be used with the butter in quantity according to taste.

There are many points to remember in making pastry. In the richest crust the quantity of butter should never exceed the quantity of flour. For ordinary pastry half the weight is sufficient. Some people prefer that the butter be mingled with a small quantity of fine lard—arguing that the latter adds to the lightness of the pastry. Pastry should be baked in a 'quick' oven, till risen and set, then in a moderate oven till slightly browned. Pies should have an air hole in the centre of the pastry to allow steam to escape. Eggs may be added to enrich pastry but liquids of other sorts must be avoided or used most sparingly.

PUFF PASTRY *c.* 1825

Weigh out equal quantity of butter and fine flour, just as much as you require of both. Mix a little of the butter into the flour with fingers, then add water, using as little as possible, just enough to make a stiff but light paste. Roll paste out on a floured baking board and slice the remainder of butter all over it. Fold in three and roll out. Fold in three again, and roll out, then touch it no more than can be avoided.

SHORTCRUST *c.* 1830

Rub twelve ounces of butter lightly into one pound of flour and mix to a paste with as little water as possible. Roll it out thinly on a floured board and use as required. Bake in a moderate oven.

A GOODLIE PYE *c.* 1600

Take small chickeyens, break their leggs and brest bones. Make of pastrie the best. Then lay the chickeyens side by side on the pastry *after filling their bellies full of bredcrumbs mixed with fresh butter, parsley, thyme, pepper and salt*, wrap pastry over them, wetting and moulding the edges together. Bake in a Dutch oven before the fire, turning occasionally, till pastry is golden, then serve in a deep oval dish, and hand round this Egg and Wine Sauce in a sauceboat along it: Mix six beaten egg yolks with white wine, vinegar, pepper, salt, ground cinnamon, sugar and rosewater to taste, and cook till sauce thickens.

As Dutch ovens are no longer used, bake as you would chicken pie in a hot oven, 475 F., till pastry is risen and set, then lower to fairly slow, 325 F., and finish cooking. It would be wise to cook sauce in a double boiler. Be sure to stir constantly, and be careful not to add more than a drop or two of rosewater, one knob of sugar and a tiny pinch of cinnamon. Sharpen with the vinegar and flavour to taste with the wine. E.C.

ANIMATED PIES

Notes made out of an Ancient book by Myself
VICTORIA, 1835

No Coronation or great Royal Feast was complete in the old days without an 'Animated Pye'. As the name suggests, this pie contained living things such as thrushes, blackbirds and hares who escaped helter-skelter when the imprisoning pastry was cut.

But the 'Animated Pye' which history relates was served at the Coronation banquet of Henry the Seventh contained even a more exciting filling. When the moment arrived for what was given out as 'A Goodlie Custard Pye' to be served, a tremendous dish, broad and deep, was carried in by four strong men 'richle clad in red and gold' who placed it upon the King's table. His Majesty cut the first slice when lo! and behold! out flew fifteen pigeons followed by an ugly hunchback! Whereupon the lords and ladies laughed mightily.

This custard pie incident is introduced in the play 'All's Well That Ends Well', and the story always provided a favourite joke for Queen Elizabeth the First and her courtiers, who often described a man who was enmeshed too closely in a woman's charms—or arms—as being 'like the dwarf in the pie'.

There is another story of an Animated Pye incident which runs like this: It is supposed to have taken place at an entertainment given by Henry the Seventh. 'A vast dish, broad and deep, filled with goodlie custards was carried by strong men and set upon ye table, and when the courtiers were busily engaged in gulping down the food, the King's Jester jumped into the custarde and swam therein, bespattering the lords and ladies to their high delight and entertainment.' It is more likely that this was the incident Shakespeare referred to in 'All's Well That Ends Well' in the following passage: 'You have made shift to run into—boots, spurs and all, like him that leaped into the custard.'

DUKE OF SUSSEX'S PIE *c.* 1845

'BIG DUCK PIE' (*In Queen Victoria's handwriting*)

Bone a fowl, and a very large duck, wash them and season with salt, pepper, allspice and mace. Boil a calf's tongue pickled red, till tender, and put inside the fowl, and put the fowl inside a large duck. Lay duck inside a large pie dish, and fill in round the duck with rich forcemeat. Then cover with a pie crust, and bake in a hot oven to start with, then a slow.

EDWARD THE SEVENTH'S STEAK AND KIDNEY PUDDING c. 1905

Cut three pounds of very lean beef into small pieces, one-third of an inch thick. Season with salt, pepper and nutmeg, some bay leaves, one laurel leaf, a little finely-chopped onion and parsley, and a small pinch of thyme and sage. A hint of garlic is permitted. Take a pudding dish or basin. Line with a firm layer of suet dough [see the Royal Suet Pudding recipe, p. 72] and garnish the bottom and sides of the basin with the slices of beef. In the middle put one pound of beef, mutton or veal kidney, cut up and seasoned like the beef. Add just sufficient water to cover meat. Close up basin with a layer of the same dough, pinching it together with the lining all round the basin to make it adhere closely, after brushing the edges with water. This done, cover the basin with a buttered and flour-dredged napkin, tied round beneath the lip of the basin with a string. Cook for 5 hours in boiling water, then remove napkin. Pin a fresh folded one round. Stand basin on a plate. Serve from basin.

PATTIES A LA REINE c. 1903

> ¾ lb puff pastry
> 1 beaten egg
> ½ pint diced cooked chicken, tongue
>   and mushrooms
> ½ pint Béchamel or Velouté Sauce

Roll pastry to a quarter of an inch in thickness. Take two round cutters, one three inches and the other two inches across. Cut out rounds with the larger cutter, then place the smaller cutter on the centre of these and cut nearly through them. (Dip cutters in hot water before using so that they may cut clean.) Brush beaten egg over rounds. Lay a little apart on a wet baking sheet, and bake in a hot oven. When cooked, remove the centre tops carefully. Heat the chicken mixture in the sauce. Fill cases with mixture. Place lids on top. Serve on a hot dish lined with a lace paper doiley.

AN EXCELLENT BEEF STEAK PIE c. 1899

Take the undercut of a tender sirloin of beef, and cut into suitable pieces for a beef steak pie. Season with pepper and salt. Dip in flour. Put a layer of prepared steak in the bottom of a pie dish, and a layer of good fresh oysters with their liquor on top, and keep on with the layers till the dish is full. Then add some freshly-made gravy, and one or two slices of butter, and cover dish with puff paste, lining the inside edge of the rim and the rim as well. Bake quickly till crust has risen, then slowly, in all for about two and a quarter hours for a decent-sized pie.

PAYN PUFF *c.* 1554

A favourite of Queen Mary the First of Scotland

Take male marrow [marrow bones]. Take therefrom the fat, add thereto powder of gynger, sugar, the yolkes of six egges, minced dates, raisens of Corance,* then stew slowly in a potte. Make goodlie coffyns of pastrie and when the mess of stew be cooked place the same therein.

I should advise mixing the fat, dates, currants, sugar and ginger to taste first in a double boiler. Stir slowly for a few minutes, then draw pan to the side. Add egg yolks. Stir till thick, and fill into little pastry cases. This sounds like the forerunner of mince pies. E.C.

PIE A LA DON PEDRO *c.* 1896

Loin of mutton
4 slices of raw ham
4 peeled onions
1 sprig of parsley
Salt and pepper to taste
3 or 4 lbs finely mashed potatoes

Divide mutton into cutlets. Cut ham into small squares and fry very lightly in a stewpan. Remove ham. Slice and add onion. Fry in ham fat without burning, until brown, then remove also. Now add cutlets and cook, turning frequently

*Raisins of Corance—currants (raisins of Corinth).

till brown, adding a pat of butter if there is not enough ham fat to sear them. Return onion to pan, add parsley and a very little salt, pepper and just enough water to keep meat from burning. Simmer slowly till tender when have potatoes ready boiled in salted water and finely mashed. Add a large pat of butter and pepper and salt to taste. If liked, also a little hot milk. Beat till creamy. Put meat with ham, onions and gravy in a pie dish. Cover with mashed potato. Dab with bits of butter and bake till crisp and golden on top.

PIGEON PIE c. 1865

In Queen Victoria's handwriting

Cut off the pinions and necks of pigeons. Season both inside and out with pepper and salt, then put a piece of fresh butter in the belly of each bird. Place a tender rump steak at the bottom of the dish, lay the pigeons upon it, place the necks, pinions, gizzards, livers etc in the centre. Cover the whole with rich shortcrust and bake.

PLOVERS' EGGS IN ROYAL FASHION
c. 1902

PASTRY: $\frac{1}{4}$ lb flour
Pinch of salt
2 ozs butter
1 egg yolk

FILLING: 6 ozs cooked chicken
$\frac{1}{2}$ gill cream
1 oz panada
Salt and cayenne pepper to taste
8 plovers' eggs
1 truffle

Sift flour with salt into a basin. Rub in butter. Stir in egg yolk and a few drops of water. Roll out. Carefully line eight to ten tartlet tins with crust. Prick insides with a fork. Bake in a hot oven, 450 F, until pale gold. Remove cases to a wire rack to cool. Pound chicken meat in a mortar with pestle until into a smooth paste. Gradually beat in cream, panada, and salt and cayenne pepper to taste. Rub through a fine sieve. Lightly poach the eggs in slightly salted water. Carefully line each tartlet case with a little of the purée. Trim eggs. Slip one into each case. Cover completely with purée, shaping it up to a dome in the centre. Place a star cut from truffle on the top of each. Sprinkle round the sides with equal quantity of fresh breadcrumbs and grated cheese. Bake in a hot oven, 450 F, for two or three minutes.

PRINCE OF WALES' SAVOURY PIE
c. 1930

Cut up two pounds of rump steak in collops the size of an apple. Trim off fat, skin and sinew. Season with pepper and salt, and fry till brown on both sides in one ounce of butter, first melted. Shake in three tablespoons of flour. Add a dozen freshly-opened oysters and their liquor, a little vinegar and mushroom sauce, a little chopped onion, a piece of bay and laurel leaf to taste. Turn into a pie dish and leave till cold. Cover with rough puff pastry. Make a hole in the centre. Ornament with pastry leaves and brush lightly over the top with beaten egg, but do not allow egg to touch the cut edge of the pastry. Bake as usual.

ROOK PIE c. 1831

6 young rooks
½ lb rump steak
Salt and pepper to taste
Pinch of grated nutmeg
Pinch of ground mace
½ pint rich beef stock
½ lb unsalted butter
¾ lb puff pastry

Pluck, skin and clean rooks, taking care not to break the gall as it would make them very bitter. Soak in cold salted water for two hours. Dry thoroughly. Placing birds on their breasts, with a sharp knife, remove backbones. Place rump steak in the bottom of a greased pie dish. Insert pie cup or funnel if required. Season birds well with salt, pepper and spices. Pack them closely over the steak. Pour stock over the birds. Slice butter thinly and lay all over the rooks. Cover with a paste made of flour and water. Bake in a moderate oven, 350 F, for two hours. Stand for twenty-four hours, then remove paste and cover with puff pastry in the usual way. Make a hole in the centre. Bake in a moderately hot oven, 375 F, for half to three-quarters of an hour. Serve hot or cold.

To Vary: Substitute bacon or ham for the rump steak. Tuck six forcemeat balls in between birds and cover with bacon or ham.

ROYAL SUET PUDDING *c.* 1905

Found in connection with Edward the Seventh's Steak and Kidney Pudding

> 1 lb sifted flour
> 1 lb fresh, finely-chopped suet
> $\frac{1}{4}$ oz salt

Moisten dry ingredients with sufficient water to make a thick paste. Cut the paste into portions weighing about one ounce each and roll into balls. Put these into a *sauté* pan containing boiling liquor and allow to cook for one and a half hours. Drain the dumplings and arrange round stewed meat. The same paste should be used for covering meat puddings.

SMALL BIRD PIES *c.* 1712

A DISH OF LARKS, SPARROWS AND BLACKBIRDS

Make some mutton broth from lean mutton. Allow to get quite cool, then skim off all fat. Now par-boil prepared small birds in slightly salted water, then put them in a pipkin. Cover with mutton broth, add a blade of mace, an whole

pepper, marigold leaves, barberries, rosewater and mary-
bones or sweet butter. Place lid on pipkin. Cook birds till
tender, then lay them on soppes of toasted bread on top of a
slice of grilled bacon, beside an oyster. The oyster could have
the bacon wrapped round it and the two grilled together as
for Angels on Horseback. Allow one slice of bacon and one
oyster to each bird.

VENISON PIE *c.* 1839

> 1 lb shoulder of venison
> 2 chopped shallots
> Salt and pepper to taste
> 1 blade of mace
> 3 allspice berries
> 1 tablespoon port wine
> 1 pint veal stock
> Raised pie crust
> Wine gravy

Remove skin from venison, and cut meat into cubes. Place in
a saucepan. Add shallots, salt and pepper to taste, mace, allspice berries, port wine and enough of the stock to cover the
meat. Cover closely. Stew very gently until almost tender,
in three and a half hours. Remove from heat. Place meat in a
basin. Moisten with a little of the gravy. Leave until cold.
Line raised pie tin with hot raised pie crust. Fill with the
meat. Cover with remainder of pastry and ornament. Bake
in a hot oven for twenty minutes, then reduce heat and bake
in a slow oven for two hours and forty minutes. Remove
ornament from top, and pour the gravy through a funnel into
the hole in crust, then replace ornament. Leave until cold.

¶ To Make Wine Gravy: Strain half a pint of
venison stock into a saucepan. Add one tablespoon port wine,
the strained juice of a small lemon, one ounce of butter
kneaded into one ounce of flour. Stir until boiling. Simmer
gently for two or three minutes, then cool before adding to
pie.

c*

WILLIAM THE FOURTH'S RUFFS *c.* 1835

Mash some freshly boiled potatoes till smooth. Add equal
quantity of flour. Mix well, then moisten to a soft dough with
beaten egg. Cut small pieces of raw mutton or steak into
small very thin slices. Season highly with pepper and salt to
taste. Turn pastry on to a lightly floured board. Roll out very
thinly. Cut into rounds. Place a piece of meat in each.
Flavour with a little finely minced onion if liked. Brush edges
with water. Fold sides to centre. Twist together. Fry in
smoking hot fat till crisp and golden. Drain well.

WINDSOR MUTTON PIES *c.* 1911

One of the favourite pies served at Royal tables today is a
small mutton pie made from a recipe of the late Monsieur
Henry Cédard, who was Maître Chef to George the Fifth.
These pies, which are very small, are also very popular with
guests at Royal Balls.

> 1 lb lean loin of mutton
> 1 dessertspoon minced parsley
> 2 tablespoons minced mushrooms
> 1 heaped tablespoon minced shallot
> Salt and pepper to taste
> Mutton gravy to moisten
> Shortcrust pastry cases

Cut mutton into very small squares. Place in a basin. Mix
with parsley, mushrooms, shallot, salt and pepper to taste,
and mutton gravy to moisten. Fill lined tartlet tins with
prepared mixture. Brush rims with cold water. Cover with
thin rounds of shortcrust to fit. Press and pinch round the
edges with forefingers and thumbs. Brush with beaten egg.
Make a small hole in centre of each to let the steam out. Bake
in a hot oven till pastry is risen and set, then lower to
moderate and bake till brown. Serve at buffet parties or high
tea, or include in luncheon and picnic baskets.

THE SWEET COURSE

THOUGH many of the desserts that were relished in the Middle Ages are never served at the Court today quite a number have survived the passage of the years. You are just as likely to find the modern version of a fruit foule on the royal menus as a mousse. Some of the desserts that figure at family meals are cabinet, semolina and treacle puddings.

Cherries have been popular with members of the British Royal family since the day on which Queen Elizabeth tasted some preserved cherries, presented to her as a New Year's gift, by one of her Maids of Honour. So delighted was the Queen with what was to her a new fruit, that it is said she never rested until the first cherry orchard* in England was planted under her direction in Kent. As the orchard covered thirty acres, Her Majesty must have eaten cherries to her heart's content as soon as the trees began to bear. Certainly, cherry pie was always a prominent dish at all her banquets from that time onwards.

Queen Henrietta Maria, Queen Anne and King George the Third evidently shared Elizabeth's fondness for cherries, for all three have been recorded as claiming cherries to be the

*Some authorities claim that cherries were grown in England before Elizabethan days.

finest of all the fruits, and cherry pie the most delicious of all
the sweets prepared in the Royal households.

Queen Victoria also placed her seal of favour upon the
cherry. When, as a girl of eighteen, she was asked to name
some of the dishes she would like to find on the menu of her
Coronation Banquet, she replied, 'Roast Chicken and Cherry
Tart'. It was noticed that the young Sovereign asked for a
second portion of the cherry tart and took with it a lavish
helping of whipped cream. Cherries always remained Queen
Victoria's favourite fruit for tarts. Before her Coronation she
gave orders that cherry pie or cherry tart should always find
a place of honour at her table, and that when fresh cherries
were not available, steamed puddings containing glacé
cherries should be served. Edward the Seventh inherited
his mother's taste for cherries, and he also had a liking for
cherry brandy. His grandson, the Duke of Windsor, when he
deigned to take tea away from home, is said to have selected
cherry tartlets after buttered toast. There used to be a little
Salon de Thé in the Rue de Rivoli, facing the Tuileries
Gardens, in Paris, where I am told His Royal Highness
indulged this fancy when in France.

Many sweets are associated with Royal names. Queen
Charlotte, wife of 'Farmer George', is reported to have given
her name to Apple Charlotte. Charlotte Russe is a rich
relation of Apple Charlotte, but bears little resemblance to it.
The most modern form of this sweet is Charlotte Princess
Marina created by C. Manzini. 'Line a charlotte mould with
chocolate fingers. Fill centre with *chocolat bavarois* (Bavarian
chocolate cream) and add chopped crystallized fruit and nuts
to taste. Pipe Chantilly cream between the fingers.'

Prince Albert gave his name to two puddings. Both are a
rich brother of the well-known 'Snowdon Pudding'.

¶ PRINCE ALBERT PUDDING (1): Beat six ounces of
fresh butter to a cream. Stir in half a pound of castor sugar
by degrees, mixed with the yolks of five eggs. When well
blended, stir in half a pound of sifted flour, half a pound of
chopped stoned raisins, one ounce of chopped candied lemon
peel, a pinch of salt, and a good glass of brandy. Beat egg

whites to a stiff froth, and fold into mixture. Pour into a buttered mould. Cover with buttered paper. Steam for three hours. c. 1850.

¶ PRINCE ALBERT PUDDING (2): Beat half a pound of butter to a cream. Stir in gradually half a pound of castor sugar. Beat till well mixed. Beat the yolks of five eggs. Sift half a pound of flour. Lightly stir in flour and egg yolks alternately. Add half a pound of chopped stoned raisins, quarter teaspoon ground mace, grated rind of a lemon, and mix well. Have ready a greased mould, ornamented with strips of candied peel. Beat egg whites to a stiff froth, and fold into other ingredients. Pour into a buttered mould. Cover with buttered paper. Steam for three hours. c. 1946.

Some years ago, I came across a recipe for chocolate pudding, contributed by the Queen Mother's cook, Mrs. MacDonald, to 'A Book of Empire Dinners'. It was included in the following menu for an Empire Dinner:

SCOTCH BROTH
FRIED FILLETS OF SOLE
NOISETTES OF VENISON
ROAST PARTRIDGE
CHOCOLATE PUDDING
BACON SAVOURY

¶ CHOCOLATE PUDDING: Take half a pound of chocolate and melt it gradually. Take out as much as you will require for sauce. Add four yolks of eggs to remainder in pan, with one and a half ounces of butter, a few drops of vanilla and one teaspoonful of flour. Stir over stove or hot water until thick, then add four well-beaten egg whites, and pour into a buttered mould. Cover with buttered paper. Steam for thirty to forty minutes. Serve sauce separate; add some butter to it. 1928.

¶ WILLIAM THE FOURTH'S FAVOURITE CREAM: Extract the juice from three small lemons, or two large oranges, and strain. Weigh. Measure two ounces more than the weight

of the juice in sifted sugar. Place sugar, two or three drops
orange flower water and five or six tablespoons of cold water
in a saucepan. Stir over slow heat till sugar is dissolved.
Add three stiffly beaten egg whites and fruit juice. Pour into
the top of a double boiler. Stir over hot water till thick, then
strain quickly through coarse muslin into serving dish.
c. 1834.

A CLEAR JELLY c. 1625

Take two calves feete and a shoulder of veale and set them
upon the fire in a large potte with a gallon of clear water and
a gallon of claret wyne, and let boyle till it be jellye, and then
take up and drayne it and putt thereto synamon, gynger and
sugar to taste and a little colouring.

Synamon=cinnamon. E.C.

GILT FISH IN JELLY c. 1715

Pour into two large fish moulds [presumably shaped in the
form of fish] clear blancmange, and when cold, turn out,
gild them with leaf gold or strew over them gold and silver,*
mixed, and lay them upon a soup dish, then fill it with clear
calf's feet jelly, thin enough to admit the fish to swim in it.
Lisbon or any kind of pale wine may be used instead of the
jelly.

A FLOATING ISLAND c. 1763

As made by the Cook of Queen Charlotte

(In Victoria's handwriting)

Take the whites of three egges and add to them a cup of
raspberrie jelly. Beat it till it be stiff which will be in about
an hour. Put it upon thick and beaten cream in a flat basin of
beauty. The cream should be sweetened with fine sugar.
[Castor sugar could be used nowadays.]

*I cannot decipher the word after 'silver'. It looks like 'cran'. E.C.

ORANGE CUSTARDE *c.* 1779

Boil in water till very tender the rind of a small Seville orange and beat it in a mortar till very fine, then add to it a spoonful of the best brandy, the juice of a Seville orange, four ounces of loaf sugar and the yolkes of four eggs. Beat all well together for ten minutes and then pour in by degrees a pint of boiling cream. Keep beating till cold, then put in cups and set in an earthenware dish of hot water till set, when turn out on a dish. Decorate with preserved orange and serve either hot or cold.

I would decorate with tiny stars or diamonds cut from crystallized orange fingers. E.C.

A CUSTARDE *c.* 1684

Bring a pint of cream to a boyle. When almost cold, beat the yolkes of eight eggs with a little rose water and grated nutmeg. Put to the cream and sweeten to your taste. Then strain it through a fine sieve and set it over a gentle fire, stirring it constantly till it thickens, then bake very slowly in small dishes till set.

BAKED CUSTARDE *c.* 1684

Boyle a pint of good fresh cream with some mace and cinnamon to taste and a laurel leaf, and when cold, mix with it four yolkes and two whites of eggs, a little rose and orange flower water and sack, grated nutmeg and sugar to taste. Pour into cups and bake.

A QUIRE OF PAPER *c.* 1569

Take three tablespoonfuls of fine flour, one pint of cream, six eggs, three tablespoonfuls of sack, one of orange flower water, a little sugar, half a nutmeg, grated, and half a pound of butter. Melt butter and leave till cold, but not solid. Gradually stir in flour, then remaining ingredients in order given. Beat till blended. Melt a nutmeg of butter in a hot amulet [omelette] pan. Run in batter as thinly as possible. Fry till just coloured, then turn and fry on other side. And so do with all the fine pancakes.

A STAPLE ROYAL PUDDING *c.* 1530

This is a pudding usually baked in the royal kitchens in winter time. The recipe has been handed down from the days of Henry the Eighth. I understand it has borne different names throughout the centuries, but the recipe remains the same. E.C.

Take half a pound of almonds, and beat them fine with a few drops of sweet water. [This means distilled water.] Add orange flower water to taste and one pint of rich cream. Warm the cream and melt in it half a pound of fresh butter before adding to the almonds, then stir in a pinch of salt, and powdered sugar and grated nutmeg to taste. Lastly, add the beaten yolks of six eggs. Beat all up together and pour into a shallow dish lined with fine puff pastry. The oven must not be too hot. Dust fine sugar upon it before serving.

This is really an open tart. Bake pastry case in a hot oven, before filling, then fill and bake at 325 F, till filling is set. E.C.

A GLORIOUS RICE PUDDING *c.* 1840

A good rice pudding must ever have half a pound of fresh butter, three-quarter pound of sugar, seven eggs, and three spoonfuls of sack. [In modern cookery, Madeira or some such wine would suit.]

AMULET (*Omelet*) *c.* 1570

Put six yolkes of eggs in a basin with six ounces of pounded sugar, a tiny pinch of salt, a tablespoonful of fine Hungarian flour, and orange flower water, grated lemon rind, grated orange rind, and vanilla, ratafia, or cinnamon to taste. Mix these ingredients up with a broad wooden spoon into a

creamy batter, and then mix in lightly and quickly the
frothed whites of nine eggs. Fry in butter in a hot omelet pan.

AN OPEN CHERRY TART *c.* 1842

Line an open tartlet tin with rich shortcrust, prick the pastry
and cook till brown and crisp. Wash and stalk a pound of
cherries, and then drop them into a syrup got from boiling a
quarter pound of loaf sugar in a quarter pint of water for ten
minutes. Simmer cherries very slowly in syrup till tender,
then strain off berries. Return syrup to pan, add a leaf of
French gelatine which has been softened in tepid water. Stir
till gelatine is dissolved, but not over the fire. Cool a little,
arrange cherries in pastry case, and spoon over the syrup.
If liked, add a few drops of maraschino to the syrup before
pouring over fruit.

CABINET PUDDING *c.* 1849

Lay in a pie dish six small sponge cakes with one glass of
Madeira to soak them, then fill the dish with a rich custard,
then strew over the top as many ratifias as you can put to
lay nicely over.

CHERRY PUDDING *c.* 1699

Take cherries, red or white, and boyle them in good red wine
[claret], then add to them ye yolkes of eggs and a lump of
swete butter and some morsels of white bread, and bake or
boil the same.
*This dish of cherries has been served at Coronation banquets in
bygone days. E.C.*

CRUSADES *c.* 1845

Cut slices of stale bread half an inch thick. Cut out as many
rounds as are required, three inches in diameter. With a
smaller cutter one and a half inches in diameter, cut half way
through each round of bread. Fry in unsalted butter until
golden brown. Drain on absorbent paper. With the point of a

knife, lift out each centre piece, leaving hollows in the
centres. Fill with apricot jam or marmalade. Press each lid
on top of filling. Dredge lightly with almond, lemon or
vanilla flavoured sugar. Reheat in oven. Serve on a hot dish
covered with a folded napkin.

DUKE OF CUMBERLAND'S PUDDING
c. 1746

Mix three ounces of grated bread with three ounces of
currants, washed and dried, three ounces of finely-shredded
beef suet, three ounces of chopped apples, three ounces of
lump sugar, a saltspoonful of grated nutmeg, a pinch of salt,
a saltspoonful ground mace, the rind of half a lemon grated,
and one and a half tablespoonfuls minced candied mixed peel.
Stir all these ingredients well together, then beat in three
eggs. Put in a buttered basin. Cover very tightly with a
floured cloth, and boil steadily for three hours. Serve with
custard sauce, flavoured with lemon juice.

ALMOND FLUMMERY c. 1670

Boil half a pound of hartshorn shavings in two quarts of water
till it reduces to one quart. Put a little isinglass into it as it
boils. Let it stand till it is cold, then add half a pint of cream,
two ounces of pounded almonds, and half a pound of loaf
sugar. Set it over a slow fire, stirring it till it is ready to
boil, then take it from fire. Keep stirring till it is almost
cold. Strain into dish and stick on top with blanched almonds.

OLD-FASHIONED FLUMMERY c. 1695

Cleanse and put four calf's feet into a gallon or six quarts of
water along with half a pound of hartshorn shavings. Boil for
four hours, then strain it into another pan and skim it clear.
Blanch and beat a quarter pound of almonds and half a pound
of loaf sugar, then mix altogether and heat up over the fire till
very hot, but do not boil. Remember to keep stirring till
almost cold, and afterwards, strain off into a pan, and let it

stand for half an hour before pouring into cups. Do not allow any of the sediment to go into the cups. When cold, loosen edges of flummery and turn out.

KING SOLOMON'S TEMPLE IN FLUMMERY *c.* 1819

Copied in Queen Victoria's handwriting and signed VICTORIA, 1836

Having divided a quart of stiff flummery in three parts, colour one part pink with a little bruised cochineal steeped in French brandy. Scrape an ounce of chocolate, dissolve it in a little strong coffee, and mix it with another part of the flummery for a light stone colour. Have the last part white. Then wet the temple mould and fit it in a pot so that it will stand even. Fill the bottom of the temple with red flummery for the steps, the four points in white, and fill it up with chocolate flummery, and let it stand until the next day. Then loosen it round with a long pin. Shake it loose very gently, and it will turn out. Stick sprigs of flowers upon the top of every point. This will strengthen the shape and give it a pleasant appearance. Lay round it rock candy sweetmeats for garnish.

No need now to bruise cochineal and steep it in brandy—just buy the liquid colouring. E.C.

TO MAKE FLUMMERY *c.* 1810

Put an ounce of bitter and an ounce of sweet blanched almonds into a basin, pouring boiling water over last mentioned in order that their skins may be quickly removed. Throw the almond kernels into cold water then take them out. Beat them in a marble mortar with a little rosewater to keep them from oiling, then put them into a pint of calf's feet stock. Sweeten it with fine loaf sugar and when it boils, strain it through a piece of fine muslin or gauze. As soon as a little cold add thereto a pint of rich and very fresh and thick cream, and stir often till thick and quite cold. Wet moulds in cold water, pour in the flummery, and let moulds stand six hours before turning out. If the flummery is made stiff, wet the moulds and it will turn out without putting them into warm water which spoils their brightness.

FOR A TANSEY *c.* 1712

Beat the yolks of thirteen eggs, and place them in a saucepan along with a pint of spinach juice, a grated nutmeg, or less if preferred, nine ounces of castor sugar, four ounces of fresh butter, nine ounces of Naples biscuits, a little tansey juice, gained by pounding some tansey in a stone mortar and one quart of milk or part milk and part cream. After stirring for a few moments, flavour to taste with orange flower water, and stir in very gradually a glass of brandy. Lastly, stir in the stiffly-whisked egg whites, and when thick, remove from fire, then put into a dish lined with shortcrust, and partly baked. Cook till tansey is ready in a moderate oven, without burning the pastry.

GOOSEBERRY FOULE *c.* 1567

Take a quart of gooseberries and scald them tender, and drain them well from the water through a cullender, and with the back of a spoon force the best part of them through the cullender, and then take a quart or three pints of new cream and also six eggs, yolks and whites, and add them to the cream; some rose water and sugar, and sweeten according to your palate. Set all on a gentle fire, and stir it till you see it of a good thickness. Then take it off and cool it a little, put it into white earthenware cream bowls, and when it is cold, serve it to the table.

HER MAJESTY'S OPEN TART 1840

A favourite open tart of Queen Victoria's

Boil one large carrot well. When cold, pound it in a mortar and rub through a sieve. Mix with grated biscuits, half a pound of melted butter, a pinch of salt, and sugar, sack and grated nutmeg to taste, also orange flower water to taste, six yolks of eggs, and three whites of eggs, beaten to a stiff froth. Have ready a dish lined and rimmed with pastry and cooked till almost ready with rice in the centre to keep pastry from rising in the middle. Throw out the rice. Gently pour the filling into the pastry-lined dish. Garnish quickly with peeled sections of orange. Sprinkle them with castor sugar. Bake half an hour in a moderate oven till filling is cooked and pastry golden.

I should use crushed macaroons and two crushed ratafias for the grated biscuits. Place a buttered paper over the filled tart for the first ten minutes. E.C.

JAUNE MANGE *c.* 1800

Boil one ounce of isinglass in three-quarters of a pint of water till melted, then strain it and add the juice of two Seville oranges, quarter pint of white wine, the yolkes of three eggs, beaten and strained, and powdered sugar to taste. Stir it over a gentle fire till it almost boils up. Leave till cold then pour into a mould. (If there should be any sediment take care not to pour it in.) If you pour a little into a number of teacups instead of a mould the jaune mange, when turned out, will look almost like poached eggs.

MOONSHINE

Copied by Queen Victoria, and dated Kensington Palace, 1833

Take a tin the shape of a half moon, and as deep as a half-pint basin, and another in the shape of a large star, and two or three smaller stars. Boil two calf's feet in a gallon of spring water till reduced to a quart. Strain it off when cold. Skim off the fat, and sweeten half the jelly to palate with sugar. Beat up the whites of four eggs. Stir with remainder of jelly over a slow fire till boiling and then run through a flannel bag till clear. Put it in a clean saucepan. Take half an ounce of blanched sweet almonds, beaten till fine in a mortar, and mixed with two spoonfuls of rosewater and orange flower water. Strain through a coarse cloth. Mix it with the jelly and four spoonfuls of fresh and thick cream, and stir all together till it boils. Then have ready the dish it is intended for. Lay the tin in the shape of a half moon in the middle, and the stars around it, with little weights on the tins to keep them in their places. Now pour the blancmange into the dish. When quite cold, take out the tins and fill up the vacancies with the calves' feet jelly. If you like, you can colour the blancmange with cochineal and chocolate to look like the sky, and the moon and the stars will then shine the brighter. Garnish with rich candied sweetmeats round the dish.

This sweet would be improved if the jelly were flavoured with lemon juice. E.C.

OLD-FASHIONED CHERRY PYE *c.* 1704

Stew the cherries till partially cooked. Then break into them five eggs, and add the juice of one lemon, and some sweet butter. Place in a piedish, cover the rim first with rich short-crust and then the top and then bake.

PANCAKES *c.* 1840

As cooked at the Palace

Put into a bowl one pound of sifted flour, six ounces of powdered sugar (less a heaped tablespoonful), and a pinch of table salt. Dilute with ten eggs and one quart good creamy milk, added slowly by degrees. Flavour with one heaped tablespoonful of orange or vanilla sugar. Beat till batter is smooth, then melt a piece of butter in a tiny omelette pan and fry a large spoonful at a time, over a very clear fire. When golden on one side, fry on other, then remove from pan with a flat knife and sprinkle with castor sugar, or spread with jam or syrup and roll up. They are usually served on a dish containing a pancake drainer to allow of all grease being removed.

You can vary the pancakes by using all the sugar and only seven gills milk, and by flavouring the batter with a quarter pint of brandy, kirsch or rum, instead of the flavoured sugar, or you can use all the milk and all the sugar and flavour with grated almonds, grated lemon peel or crushed almonds. If liked, a large omelette pan can be used and several pancakes can be cooked at once. Half this quantity is enough for an average number of people.

POOR KNIGHTS OF WINDSOR *c.* 1776

Dip slices of stale bread, cut half an inch thick, in white wine or milk sweetened with sugar, to cover. Lift each out very carefully with a broad-bladed flexible knife, and dip in beaten egg yolk. Fry till golden brown in a little butter or lard, then turn and fry on the other side. Drain on absorbent paper. Dish up. Place a spoonful of apricot, strawberry or raspberry jam on each.

OLD-FASHIONED TIPSY KENT SQUIRE *c.* 1850

1 lb tower sponge cake
$\frac{1}{4}$ lb apricot jam
$\frac{1}{4}$ lb greengage jam
$\frac{1}{4}$ lb strawberry jam
$\frac{1}{4}$ lb orange marmalade
1 tablespoonful castor sugar
$\frac{1}{2}$ pint Madeira or Marsala
$\frac{1}{2}$ gill brandy
$\frac{1}{2}$ gill Curaçoa
1 oz ratafias
2 ozs blanched almonds
1 pint rich custard
1 teaspoon vanilla essence

Cut the cake into five slices crosswise. Remove the top slice.

Spread one slice with the apricot jam, another with the greengage and the third with strawberry, then the last with the marmalade. Add sugar to the Madeira or Marsala. Stir in brandy and Curaçoa. Place the ratafias in a glass trifle dish. Place the bottom slice of cake on top of them. Sprinkle with a little of the wine. Cover with another slice of cake, sprinkle with the wine and so on until the cake is built up again and all the wine is used up. [Sometimes I spread the built-up cake with melted apricot jam flavoured with brandy, and spike with the blanched split almonds, or I cover with the custard, flavoured with vanilla, and decorate it with half a pint of Devonshire or whipped cream.]

QUAKING PUDDING *c.* 1698

> 1 quart cream
> 4 eggs
> 1½ teaspoons flour
> Castor sugar to taste
> Grated nutmeg to taste

Bring cream to a boil, then let it stand until almost cold. Beat eggs with the flour for fifteen minutes. Stir into the cream. Add sugar and nutmeg to taste. Tie tightly in a well-buttered pudding cloth. Boil for one hour. Turn out carefully or it will crack. Serve with melted butter, sweetened and flavoured with wine to taste.

QUEEN OF PUDDINGS *c.* 1839

> ¾ lb stale breadcrumbs
> 3 ozs butter
> 2 separated eggs
> 1 lemon
> ½ lb castor sugar
> 1 pint milk

Place the breadcrumbs in a buttered pie dish. Break the butter into small bits and tuck among the crumbs. Beat egg yolks with half the sugar and lemon juice. Bring milk to a boil with rind of half a lemon. Gradually strain into the yolks and sugar. Stir into crumbs. Bake in a moderate oven, 350 F, until firm, in about one hour. Beat egg whites to a stiff froth. Gradually beat in remainder of sugar and lemon juice. Spread a layer of apricot, raspberry or strawberry jam over the pudding. Cover with the meringue mixture. Bake in a moderate oven, 350 F, for about fifteen minutes until meringue is set. Serve with cream.

PRINCE CONSORT'S TART *c.* 1844

Mince one ounce of candied peel finely, then beat into a paste in a mortar. Line a pie dish with shortcrust. Melt half a pound of butter in a saucepan with six ounces of sugar. Mix well together. Remove to side of fire. Add three beaten egg yolks and orange peel. When blended, fill up pie dish. Cover with shortcrust. Bake in a hot oven to start with, then a slow. Can be eaten hot or cold.

QUEEN DOWAGER'S PUDDING *c.* 1912

$\frac{1}{2}$ lb unsalted butter
$\frac{1}{2}$ lb loaf sugar
6 beaten eggs
$\frac{1}{2}$ lb flour
$\frac{1}{4}$ lb currants
1 oz candied orange peel
1 oz candied lemon peel
20 drops lemon essence

Beat butter until softened. Crush the sugar with a rolling pin and gradually beat into the butter. Beat until creamy, then add a little of the egg. Sift flour. Sprinkle a dessertspoon over the egg. Beat well. Continue adding egg in this way until it is all blended in, then stir in remainder of flour and currants. Cut peels into very thin slices and add with lemon essence. Stir until blended. Beat for ten minutes. Three-quarters fill a well-buttered mould. Cover with greased paper. Steam for three hours.

QUEEN MARY PUDDING *c.* 1912

2 ozs butter
2 ozs castor sugar
4 egg yolks
1 oz minced nuts
2 bananas
2 ozs breadcrumbs
2 ozs chopped preserved ginger
   or pineapple
1 oz sultanas
2 egg whites

Beat butter to a cream. Gradually beat in sugar. Beat till fluffy. Gradually stir in egg yolks, one at a time. Add nuts [almonds or hazelnuts]. Peel and slice bananas. Add with crumbs, ginger or pineapple and sultanas. Beat egg whites to a stiff froth and fold into mixture. Sprinkle the inside of a buttered pudding mould with powdered macaroons. Pour in batter. Cover with buttered paper. Place in a baking tin containing hot water coming a third up the side of mould. Bake in a moderate oven, 350 F, for about one and a half hours. Unmould on to a hot dish. Coat with lemon custard sauce.

QUEEN VICTORIA'S FAVOURITE PUDDING *c.* 1852

½ lb shredded suet
¾ lb sieved breadcrumbs
¼ lb fine white sugar
¼ lb cleaned currants
Grated rind 1 lemon
Strained juice 1 lemon
3 beaten eggs
½ pint cream

Mix all the ingredients together in order given. Beat well for a quarter of an hour. Three-quarters fill six greased

dariole moulds. Place on a baking sheet. Bake in a moderately
hot oven, 400 F, for about a quarter of an hour.

RASPBERRY CREAM

In Queen Victoria's handwriting, dated Kensington Palace, 1836

Rub well a quart of raspberries, or of raspberry jam, through
a hair sieve, thus removing seeds and making smooth the
sugar to palate. Beat the whites of five eggs, mix well, and
stir it, one way only, over the fire, till it grows thick and
white. Strain through gauze and stir till cold. Then beat the
yolks of five eggs very well, and put in the pan with same
cream, and stir over a very slow fire till ready to boil, then
pour it into a basin to cool, and having stirred till quite cold,
put into glasses.

RIBAND JELLY *c.* 1720

Boil four calf's feet without the great bones in a pot of ten
quarts of clear spring water, with three ounces each of hartshorn and isinglass, a quartered nutmeg, and four blades of
mace, till reduced to two quarts. Strain through a flannel
bag and when it has stood twenty-four hours scrape off all
the fat very clean. Slice the jelly, add the whites of six eggs,
beaten to a froth, and boil the whole up and strain through a
flannel bag. Then pour into small tall glasses in different
coloured layers as thick as your finger. But each layer must
be set in turn before the other, only blood-warm, is gently
poured in, or the layers will all mix. To get the colours, use
cochineal for red, spinach juice for green, saffron for yellow,
syrup of violets for blue, and thick cream for white. Plain
jelly itself may be used as a colour.

ROYAL APPLE TART *c.* 1865

Take the pulp of boiled apples, just as much as you think you
will require for the pastry. Then take six egg yolks and three
egg whites and beat well. Mix apples with beaten egg and

two large spoonfuls of finely grated sweet biscuits, and sugar to taste. Beat the rind of a lemon or orange, boiled till tender, in a mortar with a quarter pound of fresh butter and mix with other ingredients. Pour into a pie dish lined with pastry, then cover with a crust as well and bake. When almost ready, remove top crust. Cover tart mixture with a layer of cream, cut top crust in leaves and arrange round dish.

REGENT'S PUDDING *c.* 1814

2 ozs stale breadcrumbs
2 ozs flour
3 ozs shredded suet
2 ozs grated coconut
1 tablespoon currants
1 tablespoon chopped raisins
1½ ozs sugar
Pinch of salt
4 beaten eggs
½ gill milk
2 tablespoons cream

Mix all the dry ingredients thoroughly together. Add eggs to milk. Stir into dry ingredients, with cream. Three-quarters fill a buttered basin. Cover with buttered paper. Steam quickly until done, in about three hours. Turn out carefully. Coat with Regent's Rum Sauce.

SOUFFLÉ MAGINAIRE or SOUFFLÉ THERESA *c.* 1709

1 pint of syrup of 32 degrees strength
15 yolks of eggs
½ pint maraschino
½ pint filtered strawberry juice
1 pinch of salt
¾ pint double whipped cream

Mix syrup into yolks of eggs, then strain it into a copper

bowl, previously warmed with hot water and wiped out. Add the liqueur, strawberry juice and salt, and briskly whisk the mixture, with the bottom of the bowl standing six inches deep in hot water, till it takes the form of a creamy batter and begins to feel tepid to the touch. Continue beating for about fifteen minutes, *out of the water*. Now, placing the soufflé case in the ice cave, gently and lightly incorporate the whipped cream and pour mixture into case, which should be deep enough to allow of its rising an inch. Before serving decorate surface with ratafias, glacé fruits and angelica.

ROYAL CHERRY TART *c.* 1838

Wash the cherries. Stalk, and put them in a pie dish. Sprinkle with two tablespoonfuls powdered sugar when half full, then cover with more cherries, piling them high up in the centre. Add half a gill cold water. Now make a rich shortcrust, using six ounces of butter to half a pound of flour, a tablespoonful of powdered sugar and a pinch of salt. Mix to a soft but dry dough with as little water as possible, and cover tart in usual way. Bake.

SOUFFLÉ PUDDING VENISE *c.* 1828

Finely pound four ounces of freshly washed, blanched almonds, and add thereto, from time to time, a few drops of fresh water. When the almonds form a smooth paste add the necessary quantity of water to them to produce a pint of almond milk. Strain through muslin, and slightly twist the latter in order to express all the contained liquid. With this almond milk, dilute three ounces of flour and three ounces of rice flour mixed in a saucepan, and take care that no lumps form. Strain through a strainer, and add five ounces of sugar, three ounces of butter and a little salt. Set the saucepan on the fire, boil, stirring constantly, and then stir briskly with a spatula until the preparation acquires the consistency of a thick paste and falls from the spatula without leaving any adhering portions. Pour paste into a basin, and continue beating in first two ounces of unsalted butter, little by little, then yolks of eight eggs, a little at a time, and two ounces of finely pounded almonds moistened with a tablespoonful of kirsch and as much maraschino, and lastly the stiffly whipped whites of five eggs. Cook in a buttered pie dish or soufflé dish in the oven and serve at once.

SPANISH PUFFS *c.* 1845

Boil a quarter of a pint of milk with a piece of butter the size of a walnut. Sweeten to taste, then stir in two spoonfuls of flour while boiling. Now beat in the yolks of two eggs, and lastly fold in the whites of two eggs, stiffly frothed. Drop in spoonfuls into boiling lard and fry till crisp and golden brown.

SULEBUBBLES *c.* 1600

'As made by Princess Victoria when she was a girl.' VICTORIA, 1835

Take half a pint of good cream, and half a pint of fresh rich milk, and put them into a dry pann, and put therein a spoonful of orange flower water and a little white wine. Sweeten with fine sugar. Beat the whites of two eggs, and put them in. Take the mill and grind it well, take off the froth with a spoon, and put it in your glasses as high as you can. If you will have it of a red colour, put in clarett instead of white wine, and a little in the bottom of the glass with a little sugar.

I do not know what a mill is in this case. I should use a whisk or a rotary beater. E.C.

SULLIBUB UNDER THE COW *c.* 1600

Pour a bottle of ale, cider or red or white wine into a china bowl. Sweeten it with sugar. Grate in nutmeg to taste. Hold the bowl under a cow and milk into the bowl until a fine froth covers the top. Strew a handful of cleaned, washed currants over the froth.

SYLLABUB *c.* 1800

Take one quart of thin cream and a pint of sack (sherry) and the juice of two lemons. Sweeten to your taste, and put in an earthen pan and whip it with a whisk. As the froth rises, take it off with a spoon and lay it in your syllabub glasses, but first sweeten some claret or sack, or white wine, and strain it and put seven or eight spoonfuls of the wine into eight glasses, and then gently lay in the froth, and serve at once.

THE PORRIDGE PUDDING

'This is a pudding I got on all Mondays when I was young.'
VICTORIA, 1834

Take half a pint of oatmeal. Boil a quart of good milk. Pour the milk scalding upon the oatmeal and let it stand all night covered. Then take the yolks and whites of eight eggs and beat very well, and put them into the oatmeal with a small stale loaf of bread, grated and sifted, three-quarters of a pound of picked raisins, and half a pound of cleaned currants. Add rose water, sugar and nutmeg to taste, and one and a half pounds of fresh suet, finely shredded. Boil this pudding in a buttered basin, covered with a pudding cloth, for four hours.

TO MAKE AN APPLE MOYSE 1540

Take one dozen apples and a citron, and roost or boile them, and drainne them through a streyner. Add the yolkes of five egges withal and as ye streyn the same, temper them with myrrh and three or four spoonfuls of damaske water [rosewater]. If ye will then season with sugar and half a dysche of fresh, sweet butter, and boyle them upon a chaffyng dysche in a platter and cast therein bysketts or synamon and gynger upon them, you can then serve them hotte.

I think you are meant to strew the top over with crushed macaroons, ratafias or sponge biscuit crumbs, or with ground cinnamon and ginger. E.C.

WINDSOR PALACE PUDDING *c.* 1847

Wash one ounce of rice in a colander by holding it under the cold water tap, then put in a pan and cover with milk. Cook till it is so soft it will beat into paste. Pare, core and slice apples. Place in a saucepan with one ounce of sugar, a teaspoonful lemon juice and a saltspoon of grated lemon rind. Cook for a few moments, stirring all the time to prevent fruit sticking to the pan. Once mixture boils up it is ready to lift, then beat rice to a paste, adding apples. Continue beating till mixture is very light, when lightly beat in the stiffly-frothed whites of four eggs. Whisk for a second, then dip a basin or mould into boiling water. Pour in mixture while mould is hot, and stand in boiling water till whites of eggs are set. When cooked, unmould on to a hot dish. Serve with custard, made from the four yolks of egg, poured round.

WHIPT CREAM (Made with Egg Whites)

Copied in Queen Victoria's handwriting and signed VICTORIA, 1836

Mix together the whites of eight eggs, a quart of thick fresh cream, and half a pint of sack. Sweeten with double refined sugar to taste, and perfume with musk or ambergris, orange or rose flowers, tying the latter if they be dried leaves, in a muslin cloth. Lay on the froth as high as possible in small and pretty glasses.

WHIPT CREAM (Made with Egg Yolks)

Copied by Queen Victoria, 1836

To a pint of new milk, add a few coriander seeds, washed and dried, a bit of lemon peel, a laurel leaf, a stick of cinnamon, four cloves, a blade of mace, and some sugar, and boil for ten minutes. Have ready in another stew pan the yolks of six eggs mixed with half a tablespoon of flour. Strain the milk into this mixture and set over a slow fire. Whisk till of a good consistency, but take care it does not curdle, and when cold it may be poured over gooseberries, currants and pies.

To Add Cream to Pies: Remove pastry cover. Cover fruit with cream. Decorate with leaves cut from cover.

To Perfume Cream for Pies. Add to Whipt Cream, when almost cold, a dessertspoonful of orange flower water, a tablespoonful of syrup of roses, and a little ambergris.

SUGGESTIONS FOR SWEETS

¶ APPLES, MARY QUEEN OF SCOTS ('Schlaffrock'— Apples in Nightgown): Peel and core apples. Fill centres with marmalade. Wrap each neatly in puff pastry and bake. c. 1568.

¶ WINDSOR APPLES: Peel and core apples. Stew gently till soft in a little sweetened water, with lid on pan. Do not let them break. Serve each on a rich croquette. Pour syrup round. c. 1897.

¶ PEACHES, ALEXANDRA: Arrange gently stewed, peeled peaches on a border of Genoese pastry. Cover with Chantilly cream. Pour strawberry sauce round. c. 1905.

¶ PEACHES, CHANTILLY: Peel and poach gently in a little thin syrup until soft but unbroken. Leave till cold, then arrange round strawberry ice cream. Cover with Chantilly cream. Decorate with a crown of piped red currant jelly. Place a crystallized violet on top. Sometimes, the peaches are placed round vanilla ice cream, covered with a purée of fresh strawberries, and garnished crystallized rose leaves. c. 1888.

¶ REGENT'S PETIT FOURS: Cut Genoese pastry into fancy shapes. Decorate each with a star of pineapple butter icing. Ice with *fondant* icing flavoured with pineapple essence. c. 1820.

¶ PRINCE OF WALES' FLAN: Fill a flan case with almond cream and bake. When cold, cover with Chantilly cream and decorate to taste. c. 1928.

¶ REGENT'S CREAM: Flavour a rich custard with maraschino and crushed ratafias. Bake in a charlotte mould. When turned out, garnish with halved, stewed [or tinned] apricots, and glacé cherries. Mask with apricot sauce. Serve at once. c. 1819.

¶ REGENT'S CREAM, MERINGUES: Follow previous recipe, but when ready to serve, cover with meringue and 'set' under the grill. c. 1819.

¶ ROYAL APRICOTS: Line a jelly mould with jelly flavoured with any liqueur. Arrange a layer of apricots round. Fill up with creamed *bavarois*, flavoured with purée of apricots. When set and chilled, turn out on to a base of iced Genoese pastry. Decorate with chopped blanched pistachio nuts and cream. c. 1875.

¶ VICTORIAN APRICOTS: Arrange stewed [or tinned] apricots on individual portions of shortcrust, or in baked shortcrust cases. Mask with apricot sauce. Garnish with chopped, blanched pistachio nuts. c. 1856.

¶ ROYAL PINEAPPLE: Carefully scoop out fruit from a pineapple. Fill hollow with sliced, fresh peaches and strawberries flavoured with kirsch to taste. c. 1903.

¶ VICTORIAN CROUTES: Arranged browned *brioche croutes* in a circle. Fill centre with stewed cherries and chestnuts. Mask *brioche* with apricot sauce, flavoured with rum. Serve hot. c. 1863.

¶ ALEXANDRA COUPE: Vanilla ice cream, flavoured with fresh strawberry purée. Fill into *coupe* glasses. Decorate each with a star of Chantilly cream, and crystallized violets. c. 1905.

¶ ALEXANDRA ICE CREAM: Vanilla ice cream, flavoured with *noyeau*. [see page 138] c. 1905.

¶ EDWARD THE SEVENTH ICE CREAM: Make a chocolate ice cream mixture. Add crystallized cherries to taste and freeze. c. 1902.

¶ MARY QUEEN OF SCOTS ICE CREAM: Vanilla ice pudding with *anisette* mousse in the centre. c. 1569.

¶ PRINCE OF WALES ICE CREAM: Serve fresh strawberry ice cream in wafer cases. Decorate on top with Prince of Wales' feathers in Chantilly cream. c. 1930.

SAVOURIES

Savouries as known today, did not appear in the Royal menus before Georgian days. I do not know who is responsible for their introduction. Queen Victoria was very fond of marrow toasts, and Edward the Seventh of Canapés Dianes, and also of little fried or grilled oysters. He did not like them raw.

¶ Albert Croutes: Mix highly seasoned scrambled eggs with finely chopped cooked ham to taste. Arrange on ovals of toast. Sprinkle with grated cheese. Brown quickly under the grill. c. 1842.

¶ Canapes des Princes: Pieces of chicken liver cooked on skewers and served on hot buttered toast. C. 1904.

¶ Canapes Diane: Sauté small button mushrooms lightly. Roll each in a strip of bacon. Grill. Serve side by side on hot buttered toast. c. 1902.

¶ Duke of York Cornets: Roll thin slices of cold, cooked York ham each in the shape of a horn. Garnish with

chopped aspic. Serve as an hors d'œuvre, or without the aspic
as a savoury. *c. 1930.*

¶ DUKE OF YORK EGG CANAPES: Fry eggs in oil to
cover. Serve each on a round of hot buttered toast. Garnish
with grilled York ham, and pour tomato sauce round. *c. 1930.*

¶ EDWARD THE EIGHTH CANAPES: Spread cold Welsh
rarebit enriched with egg yolks and curry to taste on fingers
of toast. Dredge with paprika, or sprinkle with minced
parsley. *c. 1936.*

¶ HENRY THE FOURTH EGG CANAPES: Serve poached
eggs. Top each with a grilled mushroom. Arrange on a round
of fried bread or hot buttered toast. Mask eggs with Béarnaise Sauce. *c. 1409.*

¶ PRINCE OF WALES CANAPES: Cut puff pastry into
ovals. Bake till crisp. Leave till cold. Pipe with cream cheese,
flavoured curry to imitate the Prince of Wales' feathers.
c. 1898.

¶ QUEEN VICTORIA'S MARROW TOASTS: (This was
written in Queen Victoria's handwriting.) Get a large
marrow bone and have it well broken. Cut the marrow
extracted therefrom into small pieces, about the size of a
filbert nut, and parboil same for a minute in boiling water.
Drain instantly upon a sieve. Season with pepper and salt,
and parsley, and maybe a suspicion of shallot. Toss lightly
together and spread upon crisp slices of toast. *c. 1845.*

¶ VICTORIA CANAPES: Pound cooked ham in a mortar.
Mix to taste with *purée de foie gras.* Spread evenly on fingers
of toast. Make a Victoria cross on each with strips of anchovy
fillets. *c. 1845.*

¶ VICTORIA SANDWICHES: Mix diced lobster to taste
with highly seasoned white sauce, flavoured anchovy essence.
Use with white or brown bread. *c. 1850.*

FOIE GRAS MOUSSE *c.* 1903

Turn out a half-pound tin of *foie gras*, and remove the fat.
Slice liver. Place in a frying pan containing enough melted
butter to cover bottom of pan, a sliced carrot, sliced onion,
one dessertspoon of diced lean bacon and a small sprig of
thyme. Cook slowly for two or three minutes. Moisten with a
glass of sherry. Season with a dash of ground mace and salt
and pepper to taste. Line eight or ten tiny fluted moulds with
aspic jelly. Ornament each with a truffle. Pound *foie gras*
mixture in a mortar, then rub through a sieve into a basin.
Stir in two tablespoons liquified aspic jelly and two tablespoons dissolved meat glaze. Stir over ice until mixture
begins to thicken. Gradually add a tablespoonful more of
aspic jelly or rich veal stock. Lastly, fold in about half a gill of
whipped cream. Fill up moulds. Chill. Arrange on a dish in a
circle, standing each on a mound of aspic jelly, a little wider
than the mousses. Fill the centre of the circle with cooked
seasoned green peas moistened with mayonnaise aspic.
Garnish with sprigs of parsley and ornaments of aspic cut out
of jelly.

FRIED OYSTERS *c.* 1903

> 1 quart oysters
> 2 slightly beaten eggs
> Crumbs as required

Dry the oysters thoroughly in a clean towel. Egg and crumb.
Chill. Heat fat to between 375 and 380 F, and drop in the
oysters, a few at a time. Fry until golden brown in two to
three minutes. Drain on absorbent paper. Garnish with
lemon. (If wanted for luncheon, serve with sauce tartare.)

ŒUFS A LA REINE ALEXANDRA *c.* 1902

Roll half a pound of shortcrust out into a round about a
quarter of an inch thick. Cut into small rounds with a floured
fluted cutter. Line fluted patty tins. Prick the insides well to
prevent crust rising. Bake in a hot oven, 450 F, until pale

brown. Fill each with a trimmed, lightly-poached egg. Sprinkle a little caviare round each egg. Garnish centre of each with a small round slice of truffle. Place two narrow strips of red pepper or pimiento side by side on top of each round. Arrange on a hot dish lined with a paper doiley.

TO DRESS PIG'S PETTYTOES c. 1841

Place the heart, liver, lights and feet in a saucepan. Bring to boyle. Skim. Boyle for ten minutes, then carefully remove the heart, liver and lights. Cut into small shreds. Let the feet boyle till pretty tender, then take feet out and split each in two. Thicken the gravy with butter rubbed with flour. Add minced heart, liver and lights, salt to taste, a slice of lemon, and a tablespoon of white wine, then bring to boyle. Beat the yolke of one egg. Stir in two tablespoons of thick cream, and a pinch of grated nutmeg. Gradually stir this into the gravy. Add pettytoes. Shake over the fire, but do not allow to boyle. Remove the feet to a hot dish. Pour the sauce with the minced heart, liver and lights, into a hot dish. Lay the feet on top, skinned side up, and garnish with sippets of toast.

TOASTED CHEESE c. 1600

There are many versions of this. Some suggest spreading slices of fried bread thinly with mustard and topping it with cheese, then baking it in a hot oven for five to ten minutes. Here is an adaptation of the Elizabethan method: Melt half an ounce of butter in a small saucepan, then add a quarter pound of grated cheese. When melted, I would stir in about one teaspoonful of made mustard, about two tablespoons ale, and, when blended, pour this on to hot buttered toast.

FROM THE ROYAL CAKE
BASKET

CERTAIN birds and pies may have vanished from the Royal
table of today, but there is little change in the contents of the
cake basket. The same cakes that were enjoyed by the Tudors
and Stuarts are popular today, although sometimes in a
modernized form. In some ancient books I have read about
Tantillons. In others I have been fascinated about the
ceremony attached to the service of *Tentations*. Both seem to
me to be ancestors of the modern meringue, known in
America as a 'kiss'. When Queen Henrietta Maria was in
residence at Richmond Palace, these little cakes were always
served at her table. It was at Richmond too, that the famous
'Maids-of-Honour' which have retained their popularity
down the centuries, were first made.

Several years ago, I had the pleasure of sampling them in
the chamber where Queen Elizabeth died in the Old Palace at
Richmond. My hostess, who was an American, beguiled the
time with tales of Tudor and Stuart days: of how Philip of
Spain courted 'Bloody Mary' in the garden below, of how
Elizabeth sat at the window of the room where we had tea
and waited and waited for the ring she had given to Essex as

a pledge of her affection, promising him at sight of it a favourable hearing no matter with what offences he might be charged. But owing to intrigue, when his life was at stake, the ring never came. . . .

In the old days when the fear of poison was never absent from the minds of kings and queens, the serving of *Tentations* was accompanied by the following ceremony: at coronation feasts and at all royal banquets, the chief Lady-in-Waiting, at the conclusion of the meal, carried these little cakes on a dish to her sovereign and the chief guests. She handed them a 'faire cloth' with which they wiped their hands and mouths, then she kissed the cloth in token of fidelity and presented the little white cakes. Perhaps that is why these cakes are sometimes known as 'kisses'.

OLD RECEIPT FOR KISSES *c.* 1627

Take the whites of four eggs, beat till stiff then slowly cast into them one pot and a half pot [cup] of the finest white sugar. Mix in lightly, then fill a tablespoon with the paste, smooth with another spoon to an egg-shape, as quickly as possible, and drop each about two inches apart on a baking sheet covered with strips of stiff white paper. Sift a little sugar over each, and bake in a slow oven till light fawn. Cool a little then pass a thin knife under each. Scoop out a portion of the soft part and replace in oven to dry. Before using, fill hollows with whipped cream and put two together.

QUEEN ANNE'S FRENCH BREAD 1704

To two quarts of fine flour and half a pint of ale yeast, use one and a half pints of new milk warmed. Put the yeast into the milk. Add half a spoonful of salt, and stir it together, and strain it through a hair sieve into the flour, and make it into a little paste not kneaded, but work it gently with your hand; then warm a linen or woollen cloth very hot, and lay upon your paste, and set it to warm by the fire to raise for half an hour; then work it up lightly with your hand again, and have some wooden dishes warm, and pinch off little pieces as big as

D*

a turkey's egg; flour your dishes, and put into every dish a
piece of dough, and cover it down warm, and let it stand by
the fire a quarter of an hour; then half hour bakes it in a
pretty quick oven; while it is hot chip it.

QUEEN MARY'S TEACAKES *c.* 1691

1 quart fine flour
½ lb butter
2 eggs
2 tablespoons sugar
1 tablespoon yeast
1 pint new milk

Dry flour before the fire and rub in the butter. Beat eggs with
sugar and yeast. Pour into centre of flour, and keep mixing
well with the milk. Beat up with the hand and set, covered
with a cloth, to rise before the fire. In about half an hour
make into cakes about an inch thick. Put on a tin plate, and
set before the fire to rise for about ten minutes. Bake in a
slow oven, then butter and eat hot.

SIR WALTER RALEIGH'S
MERRY CAKES

'This was a favourite breakfast cake of Queen Elizabeth the First.'
VICTORIA, 1840

One pound of fine flour, a piece of butter the size of a filbert
nut (if larger no harm will be worked), a quarter of a pint of
cold spring water, one pinch of salt. The cook that cannot mix
these is no cook.

CHEESE CAKES

'As made for Queen Anne Boleyn'—copied by Princess
Victoria. Kensington Palace, 1836, 'from my ancient Receipt
Book.'

There were many cheese cakes made for the Queen Con-

sort of Henry the Eighth. This Queen Consort was very
partial to these cakes. A cook shop in Richmond also made
cheese cakes for her.

Put three quarts of creamy fresh milk to a quarter pint of
rennet. Let it stand in a warm place, and when set, drain it
thoroughly and mix into it with the hand half a pound of
sweet fresh butter. Sweeten to palate with fine sugar, and
add a few cleaned currants, a little citron and candied orange
and lemon peel, cut small, and an ounce of whitened and
pounded Jordan almonds. Then beat up three eggs with the
mixture. Sheet [line] the pans with fine light pastry, fill them
with the curd and bake them in a swift oven. The paste may
be made with half a pound of sifted flour, quarter pound of
fresh butter, and cold spring water, mixed lightly and rolled
out.

SMALL CRUSTS FOR CHEESE OR WINE AFTER DINNER

'These are good for dispeptics.' VICTORIA, 1836

Pull the crumb of a newly baked loaf into small pieces, put
on a baking tin, and set in a moderately heated oven till they
are of a nice brown colour.

STRATHMORE SCONES 1936

> ½ lb flour
> 2 teaspoons castor sugar
> ¼ teaspoon bicarbonate of soda
> ½ teaspoon cream of tartar
> Pinch of salt
> 1 beaten egg
> ½ teaspoon golden syrup
> Milk as required

Sift flour, sugar, soda, cream of tartar and salt into a basin.
Add two tablespoons milk to the egg. Stir in syrup. Beat till
well mixed. Make a hollow in centre of flour. Add liquid, and

enough milk to make a batter, like a very thick cream. Pour into a jug. Heat and rub a girdle, or thick frying pan, with a piece of suet. Pour batter on to girdle or into pan in rounds, keeping them at least one inch apart. Bake over a hot stove until brown below, and full of bubbles on top. Turn and brown on the other side. Serve hot with butter, or cold with butter and honey or strawberry jam.

BOSWORTH JUMBLES c. 1485

The original of this recipe is claimed to have been picked up on the Bosworth battlefield where it is supposed to have been dropped by the cook of Richard the Third.

> 6 ozs butter
> 1 lb castor sugar
> ½ lb flour
> 1 large egg

Beat butter until softened, then gradually beat in sugar. Sprinkle with a little of the flour. Add egg and sprinkle with a little more flour. Beat in egg. Add remainder of flour. Knead until smooth. Divide in small equal portions, and shape each portion into the form of a letter S. Place a little apart on a greased shallow baking tin. Chill. Bake in a moderate oven, 350 F, until pale brown in about twenty minutes.

ALMOND CHEESE CAKES c. 1845

Put four ounces of blanched and pounded Jordan almonds into cold spring water. Then beat them with rose water in a marble mortar, or wooden bowl, and add four ounces of fine sugar, and the yolkes of four eggs, beaten very well. Work it in a bowl or mortar till frothy and white. Then take half a pound of fine flour, and a quarter pound of sweet butter. Rub a little of the butter into the flour, and mix till stiff with a little cold spring water. Roll the paste straight out. Throw over it a little flour and lay over it one third of the butter in thin bits. Throw a little more flour over the butter and do so three times. Then line cheese cake tins with this. Fill them

with mixture. Dust each with sugar and put in a gentle oven
to bake.

*Ground almonds can be added to sugar instead of prepared whole
almonds. E.C.*

BALMORAL CHEESE CAKES 1850

Line patty pans with rich shortcrust, then half-fill with the
following mixture and bake in a hot oven for fifteen to
twenty minutes.

For the Filling: Beat together a quarter pound of butter and
a quarter pound of sifted sugar. Add two beaten eggs, one
ounce of stale sponge cake crumbs, a quarter ounce of cornflour, one ounce of glacé cherries, and one ounce of candied
peel, both cut up finely. Lastly, add a teaspoonful of brandy
or home-made wine and the stiffly-whipped white of an egg.
Pastry made from half a pound of flour and a quarter pound of
butter with a squeeze of lemon juice, and a little cold water,
will do for the cases. About a teaspoonful of filling should be
put in each case.

ROYAL CHEESE CAKES *c.* 1712

Mix two ounces sifted sugar with the strained juice and the
grated rind of a lemon and half an orange. Stir in two ounces
beaten butter, one ounce of crumbled sponge cake, and two
beaten eggs, and half-fill patty pans lined with pastry and
bake.

YE CHEESE CAKES BELOVED BY Y^E QUEEN ANNE BOLEYN 1510

Take three pints of sweet and new milk and boyle it and when
it boyls, put therein twelve egg yolks, but only half of the
whites, with a little salt. Stir always over the fire till it comes
to the curd. Then strain the whey from it through a fine hair
sieve. When it be drained put it into a dish, stirring in a
portion of fresh butter and a pot [cup] of thick sweet cream.

Season well with sack, rosewater, cleaned currants, cinnamon, sugar and all other spices pleasing to the taste. Half fill patty pans lined with puff pastry, and bake.

PORTUGAL CAKES *c.* 1664

'Being the cakes favoured by Queen Catherine of Braganza, the Queen Consort of Charles the Second.' VICTORIA

Mix with the hand a pound of fine flour, a pound of sifted sugar, and a pound of fresh sweet butter. Add thereto two spoonfuls of rose water, half a pound of currants, washed and dried very well, and break in ten eggs and whisk well together. If cakes are wanted very light, beat the yolks of eggs alone, and add them, then beat whites to a stiff froth, and fold them lightly in. Then butter insides of ten moulds, and fill them three parts full with the mixture, and bake in a fairly swift oven.

PRINCESS ROYAL CAKES *c.* 1920

6 ozs butter
8 ozs castor sugar
3 eggs
$\frac{3}{4}$ lb flour
$\frac{1}{2}$ teaspoon baking powder
$\frac{1}{4}$ gill milk
$\frac{1}{4}$ lb sultanas
1 oz crushed ratafias
$\frac{1}{2}$ teaspoon vanilla essence

Beat butter until softened, then gradually beat in sugar. Beat until fluffy. Add one egg at a time, beating until blended before adding next. Beat until creamy. Sift flour with baking powder. Lightly stir into batter alternately with milk. Stir in sultanas, ratafias and vanilla essence. Three-quarters fill patty tins. Place on a baking sheet. Bake in a moderate oven 375 F, for about twenty minutes. Place on a wire rack. Cover the top of each with fondant icing. Sprinkle lightly with desiccated coconut. Pipe round the edge chocolate butter crême or royal icing.

MAIDS OF HONOUR

There are many methods of making Maids of Honour. Here are two recipes for these royal cakes:

¶ FOR MODERN MAIDS OF HONOUR:1. Beat two ounces of sugar and two ounces of butter to a cream. Stir in one ounce of desiccated coconut, a beaten egg, the grated rind and strained juice of a lemon and lastly a tablespoon of cooked sago. Half-fill patty pans lined with pastry. Bake in a quick oven for about fifteen minutes. *c.* 1906.

2. Boil half a pint of milk and two tablespoons of fine white breadcrumbs together for fifteen minutes, along with two ounces of butter, grated lemon peel and sugar to taste. Then add three eggs, well-beaten, and stir mixture till quite thick. Rub through a sieve. Line small cheesecake tins with puff pastry. Half-fill with mixture and bake. *c.* 1919.

MARCHPANES *c.* 1736

$\frac{1}{2}$ lb sweet ground almonds
$\frac{1}{2}$ oz bitter ground almonds
$\frac{1}{4}$ lb castor sugar
$\frac{1}{4}$ lb sifted icing sugar

Mix ingredients in an enamel saucepan. Stir over slow heat till into a stiff smooth paste. Knead lightly into a ball on a board covered with castor sugar. Leave till cool. Roll out into a round about a quarter inch thick. Cut into fancy shapes. Pair, if liked, with apricot jam. Bake in a fairly slow oven, 325 F, till pale gold.

ROUT DROPS *c.* 1899

Clean one pound of currants and mix them with two pounds of flour, then add to one pound of butter and the same quantity of castor sugar which you have creamed together. Make into a stiff paste, with two beaten eggs, a large spoonful of orange flower water, and the same of rose water, sweet wine and brandy. Flour a baking tin to put them on and bake a very short time in a moderately hot oven, 375 F.

I would roll them out and cut them into fancy shapes before baking. E.C.

QUEEN CAKES c. 1821

Called after Queen Adelaide, Consort of William the Fourth. Copied by Queen Victoria.

Have ready one pound of loaf sugar, well sifted, a pound of fine flour, and a pound of fresh butter, and eight eggs, also half a pound of cleaned currants, a grated nutmeg, and the same quantity of ground mace and ground cinnamon. Work the butter into a cream, then gradually beat in the sugar. Beat the yolks of eggs for half an hour, and add them to the butter. Beat the whites of eggs half an hour and add them to the sugar, and then beat all together and when ready for the oven, add the currants, spices and flour. Three-quarters fill buttered queen cake tins. Dust with a little fine sugar over them and bake.

Only beat egg whites till stiff. Gem or patty tins will do to bake cakes in. E.C.

SCOTCH PETTICOAT TAILS c. 1568

Favourite cakes of Mary, Queen of Scots. She brought the recipe with her from France where the cakes were then known as Petits Gateaux Tailes.

Rub six ounces butter into one pound of flour, then mix in six ounces of powdered sugar and a teaspoonful of baking powder. Add a little water, and work into a smooth dough with the hands. Divide in two portions. Roll into round cakes about the size of a dinner plate. Cut a round cake from the centre of each with a cutter four inches in diameter, then divide the outside of each into eight. Prick all over each with a fork. Dust with the finest of sugar, and bake on buttered tins in a moderate oven for about twenty minutes, till crisp and golden. Dust with castor sugar.

SMALL CAKES MUCH ESTEEMED AT COURT *c.* 1720

Take three pounds of very fine flour, one and a half pounds of butter, and as much currants, and same of sugar; seven eggs (half of the whites taken out), and knead all well together into a paste; a little nutmeg grated, and a little rose water; so make them up about the thickness of your hand, and bake them upon a plate of tin.

TO MAKE LITTLE CAKES SUCH AS PRINCESS CHARLOTTE FAVOURED *c.* 1814

She was the daughter of King George the Fourth, and died young. Copied by Queen Victoria.

Take half a pound of fresh butter, clean from salt, and beat it well. Then break in ye yolks of four eggs, leave out the whites, then beat the butter and eggs well together, and put therein two spoonfuls of rose water. Then take the flour, well dried, and the sugar, finely sifted, and add, a little at a time, still beating. There must be half a pound of each. When the oven be ready, put them into buttered and floured panns. Put some sugar over them. Then sprinkle each lightly with ground mace. Your oven must not be hotte.

TUNBRIDGE CAKES *c.* 1780

Rub three ounces of butter into two pounds of flour. Add three ounces of castor sugar and a few carraway seeds. Wet ingredients with a little warm water, a little brandy, one egg and a little rose water. Make into a stiff paste. Roll out thin and cut the paste with the top of a wine glass. Bake on a buttered tin a little while in the oven.

Use a moderately hot oven, heated to 375 F. E.C.

TWELFTH NIGHT CAKES *c.* 1730

Make a cavity in the centre of six pounds of fine flour in a basin. Dissolve a gill and a half of yeast in a little tepid milk and work it into the centre of the flour to make a sponge. Place round it one pound of fresh butter in small lumps, one and a quarter pounds of sifted sugar, four and a half pounds of washed and dried currants, half an ounce of sifted cinnamon, quarter ounce of pounded cloves, grated mace and nutmeg to taste, and sliced candied orange, lemon and citron peel to taste. When sponge is risen, mix all together with a little warm milk. Have the hoops well prepared and buttered, and fill with the mixture, and bake them till ready. When almost cold, ice same over with sugar and water.

TUDOR ROSES 1952

    1 oz sifted icing sugar
    3 ozs butter
    3 ozs flour
    ¼ teaspoon vanilla essence
    Tiny pinch of ground mace

Beat sugar and butter till fluffy. Sift flour. Gradually beat into fat and sugar. Stir in vanilla essence and mace. Beat well. Place in a syringe or icing bag with a large rose patterned tube fixed. Force in large roses one inch apart on a greased baking sheet. Chill. Bake in a moderate oven, 350 F, for about twelve minutes. *Yield:* About three dozen.

A POUND CAKE *c.* 1838

Take one pound of butter and the yolks of eight eggs, and beat to a cream with your hand. Shake in one pound of fine sugar, and a glass of mixed brandy, and orange flower and rose water, and a little grated nutmeg. Then lastly shake in one pound of fine flour and bake in a buttered pan in the oven for two hours. You may, if you please, shake in a pound of cleaned currants, and one ounce each of citron, lemon and orange peel finely shredded and two ounces of blanched and bruised Jordan almonds.

WHIGS *c.* 1775

In the handwriting of Queen Victoria

To half a pint of warm milk, add three-quarter pound of fine flour and mix into this two or three spoonfuls of light barm. Cover it up and set it before the fire for one hour to rise. Work into the paste four ounces of sugar and four ounces of butter. Make it into whigs with as little flour as possible, and a few seeds and bake in a quick oven.

I expect seeds referred to are carraway. I should shape dough into rolls and bake them in a buttered tin. There is evidently a political joke connected with these cakes. E.C.

'A CAKE THAT WILL NOT MOULDER'
c. 1818

'This cake will keep a quarter of a year.' VICTORIA

Take four pounds of butter and work it well with the hands till in a cream. Then take a quart of ale yeast. Strain it into the butter but you must still keep working it. Then take the yolkes of ten eggs, and beat them well and put with them half a pint of rosewater, or orange flower water, and almost a quart of fresh thick cream and strain them into the butter and yeast, but not ceasing to work on the same till you put it in the hoop. Then take half a peck of the finest flour and a pound of loaf sugar beaten fine [you could use castor sugar], and a quarter ounce of ground mace. Mix this with the flour. When all is softly working, add half the flour and mix well. Then place therein six pounds of currants, well washed and dried and mingled with remainder of flour, and by degrees work all well together, the more the merryer, and work together in the hoop that the better the cake will be. The mess should stick to your hands and to the dish before it be baked. Set it in an oven from which the heat has a little fallen, and let it stand for two hours, or something more.

BRIDAL CAKE 1837

*This cake was made for the private use of Queen Victoria on her wedding day**

Two pounds of sifted sugar (loaf), four pounds of fresh butter, four pounds best white flour and a quarter ounce each of ground mace, cinnamon and nutmeg, thirty eggs, four pounds of cleaned currants, one pound blanched and pounded Jordan almonds, one pound of citron peel, one pound of candied orange peel, and one pound of candied lemon peel, all cut into slices, and about half a pint of good brandy. (A pint may be too much.) First work the butter to a cream with the hand, then beat in the sugar for fifteen minutes, and whisk the whites of the eggs to a solid froth and mix them with the sugar and butter, then beat the yolks for fifteen minutes and add them to the mixture. Likewise the flour, mace and nutmeg, and beat all well together till the oven be ready. Then mix in lightly the brandy, currants, almonds and sweetmeats. Line a 'hoop' with buttered paper, fill it with the mixture, and bake it in a brisk oven. When risen, cover it with paper to keep it from burning. Serve it iced or plain.

CAKE MUCH LIKED BY
THE PRUSSIAN KING

The King referred to was Friedrich Wilhelm the Fourth, great-grandfather of the Kaiser Wilhelm

Have ready half a pound of dried flour and one pound of beaten sifted sugar, the yolkes and whites beaten separately

* I fancy this was a private wedding cake of Queen Victoria's, for she had far more magnificent wedding cakes made by the Royal cooks. But it makes this one all the more interesting. It is known that Queen Victoria hated rich recipes, so it may be that she had a less rich wedding cake made for her own private consumption. Anyhow this is the recipe for a Bridal Cake as entered in her book. *E.C.*

of seven eggs, the juice of a lemon, with its grated peel, and half a pound of blanched almonds, ground finely with rose-water. Place the flour last into the vessel before mixing well together. Then put cake in ordinarily hotte oven.

This is evidently an almond sponge cake. Use ground almonds, and place mixture in a cake tin dusted out with equal quantities of flour or cornflour and sugar. Despite the instructions, I should beat yolks and sugar together for fifteen minutes, then add lemon, flour and almonds, and lastly fold in stiffly-whipped egg whites. E.C.

CROWN JEWEL CAKE 1953

This is a recipe I have created for a cake in honour of the Coronation of Her Majesty, Queen Elizabeth.

$\frac{1}{2}$ lb flour
$\frac{1}{2}$ teaspoon salt
$\frac{1}{2}$ teaspoon baking powder
$\frac{1}{2}$ lb butter
$\frac{1}{2}$ lb castor sugar
4 large eggs
$\frac{1}{4}$ lb halved glacé cherries
6 ozs diced glacé pineapple
2 ozs chopped glacé ginger
3 ozs sliced angelica
2 ozs minced candied citron peel
2 ozs ground almonds
Grated rind of $\frac{1}{2}$ a lemon
$\frac{1}{2}$ teaspoon vanilla essence

Grease an eight inch cake tin. Line smoothly with two layers of greaseproof paper. Sift flour, salt and baking powder. Beat butter till softened. Gradually beat in sugar. Beat till fluffy. Beat eggs. Drop a little of the egg into fat mixture. Dredge lightly with a little of the flour. Beat till blended. Repeat till all the egg is added, then lightly stir in the flour. Now mix fruit, ginger, angelica, and peel with the almonds. Stir lightly into mixture. When blended, stir in lemon rind and vanilla essence. (If not able to spare four eggs, use only three diluted

with two or three tablespoons of milk or water.) Pack lightly
into prepared tin. Hollow out centre slightly with the back of
hand. Insert in oven heated 375 F (moderately hot), and
lower at once to 325 F (fairly slow). Bake for about three and
a half hours, till dry in the centre when tested with a skewer.
Remove from oven. Stand for fifteen minutes, then turn out
gently on to a rack, base downwards. Leave for twelve hours.
Brush top with melted apricot jam. Cover top with almond
paste. Leave in a warm room for forty-eight hours. Coat
with a layer of water icing. When set, coat with royal icing.
Decorate with a marzipan crown, coloured gold with amber
or saffron colouring. Imitate jewels with silver and mimosa
balls, bits of angelica, etc. Pipe roses of royal icing round the
top and bottom edges, coloured rose pink. Decorate with
flags and silver balls.

¶ ALMOND PASTE: Mix eight ounces of ground almonds
with four ounces of sifted icing sugar and four ounces of
castor sugar. Add one teaspoon of lemon juice, a quarter of a
teaspoon of vanilla essence, two or three drops of almond
essence, and beaten egg to mix.

¶ ROYAL ICING: Made with two pounds of icing sugar,
two teaspoons of lemon juice, one teaspoon of pure glycerine,
one or two drops of blue colouring, and four egg whites.

PLUM CAKE *c.* 1806

Copied by Queen Victoria

To seven pounds of currants, add four pounds of fine flour,
six pounds of the best butter, and two pounds of blanched
Jordan almonds pounded and mixed with orange flower
water, and four pounds of eggs, but without whites, three
pounds of finest sugar, quarter ounce of ground mace, quarter
ounce of ground cloves, quarter ounce of ground cinnamon,
three large nutmegs, grated, a little ginger, half a pint of sack
[sherry], half a pint of best brandy and sweetmeats, a candied
orange, lemon and citron, cut small, the juice and rind of a

fresh lemon. Work butter to a cream before mixing in other ingredients, then beat in the sugar, and work well together. Have the eggs well beaten and strained. Work in the pounded almonds, and then the eggs, till white and thick. Add the sack, brandy and spices, shake in the flour by degrees, and put in the currants and sweetmeats as the mixture is put into the hoops. Bake directly in a quick oven for four hours. Keep beating it all the time it is being mixed, and keep the currants before the fire so that they will go warm into the cake. This quantity will bake in two hoops. One hoop will be too small for the entire mixture.

QUEEN MARY'S JUBILEE CAKE 1935

This is a recipe I created for a cake in honour of the Jubilee of Queen Mary and King George the Fifth

9 ozs butter
$\frac{1}{2}$ lb castor sugar
5 eggs
$\frac{3}{4}$ lb sifted flour
Pinch of salt
1 teaspoon baking powder
2 ozs cleaned currants
2 ozs picked sultanas
3 ozs chopped mixed peel
Pinch of ground mace
1 tablespoon sherry
3 ozs chopped glacé cherries
2 ozs chopped citron peel
1 oz ground almonds
Grated rind of $\frac{1}{2}$ a lemon
1 dessertspoon rosewater
2 ozs chopped walnuts
$\frac{1}{4}$ teaspoon vanilla essence
3 lbs of almond paste

Grease a cake tin, nine inches across. Line smoothly with five layers of greased paper. Tie a thick band of paper round the outside. Place on a bed of kitchen salt in a round baking tin. Push salt close to base. Cream butter and sugar. Beat in eggs. Sift flour with salt and baking powder. Stir into butter and sugar. Put a quarter of the mixture into a basin, and divide remainder into two. Remove half to another basin. Add currants, sultanas, mixed peel, ground mace, and half a teaspoon of mixed spice if liked, with sherry to one large portion. Place in prepared tin. Stir cherries, citron peel, almonds, lemon rind, and rosewater into other large portion. Place second large portion evenly on top of first in tin. Stir walnuts and vanilla into small portion. Spread on top. Place in oven, and bake at 325-350 F, for about two and a half hours, then test. When ready, remove from oven and stand for fifteen minutes, then turn out on to a wire rack. Leave for twelve hours. Decorate with almond paste and royal icing.

CUMBERLAND GINGER SHORTCAKE
c. 1839

This cake was sent from Cumberland every year to Queen Victoria on her birthday. The receipt is not much known beyond the county.

> ½ lb sifted flour
> Pinch of salt
> ½ teaspoon bicarbonate of soda
> ½ teaspoon cream of tartar
> Powdered ginger to taste
> ¼ lb brown sugar
> ¼ lb butter

Mix all dry ingredients together. Rub in butter. Stir well, then put into a well-buttered tin, pressing down firmly with the back of a wooden spoon. (The cake should be level and only half an inch deep.) No moistening required. Bake in a moderate oven for about half an hour.

Some recipes suggest two ounces of ginger, others two and a quarter to two and three-quarters. I find a quarter ounce makes this cake hot enough to my taste. E.C.

LORD LASCELLES'
CHRISTENING CAKE 1923

10 lbs butter
10 lbs sugar
About 120 eggs
12½ lbs sifted flour
6 lbs seedless raisins
20 lbs washed, dried currants
12½ lbs picked sultanas
3½ lbs minced orange peel
10 ozs minced citron peel
3 lbs minced lemon peel
2 lbs blanched almonds
2 lbs ground almonds
5 lemons, juice and grated rind
5 oranges, juice and grated rind

The cake was mixed and baked like any rich fruit cake. When cold, it was covered with almond paste in the usual way, and when dry with royal icing, then decorated in a dignified panelled design in which children's figures, doves and lilies, exquisitely framed in Wedgwood blue, served to lighten the chaste severity of plain surfaces unadorned by the usual cupids and artificial flowers.

INGREDIENTS FOR A DOUGH CAKE

2 lbs fresh butter
1 lb carraway seeds
4 ordinary spoonfuls good yeast
10 eggs, with 5 whites
3 large spoonfuls thick cream
Flour as required

RICE CAKE *c.* 1828

Take five ounces each of ground rice and dried flour, twelve ounces of powdered sugar, and nine eggs, well beaten. Mix well, then add the grated rind of a large lemon. Beat for thirty minutes, then bake on a greased cake tin lined with buttered paper for forty-five minutes.

QUEEN ELIZABETH'S CORONATION CAKE 1937

This is a recipe for a cake I created in honour of the Coronation of Queen Elizabeth and King George the Sixth

1 lb Australian currants
½ lb South African sultanas
6 ozs Australian raisins
¾ lb mixed candied peel
6 ozs ground cashew nuts
½ lb butter
½ lb castor sugar
10 ozs sifted flour
½ teaspoon baking powder
Pinch of salt
¼ teaspoon ground cinnamon
¼ teaspoon mixed spice
¼ teaspoon ground mace
¼ teaspoon grated nutmeg
5 eggs
1 tablespoon black coffee
1 tablespoon lemon juice
1 dessertspoon golden syrup
1 tablespoon Cyprus brandy
A little jelly
2½- 3 lbs almond paste
Royal icing

Grease a cake tin nine inches across. Line smoothly with five layers of greased paper. Tie a thick band of paper round the outside. Place on a bed of kitchen salt in a round baking tin. Push salt close to base. Clean currants and sultanas. Stone raisins. Shred peel. Place in a basin. Stir in nuts. Beat butter and sugar to a cream. Sift flour with baking powder, salt and spices on to paper. Beat eggs. Add flour and eggs alternately to butter and sugar till all egg is used up, then add coffee, lemon juice and syrup, beating constantly. Add remainder of flour alternately with fruit mixture, still beating. Add brandy. Mix well. Pour into prepared tin. Hollow out the centre. Bake in a moderately slow oven, 325 F, for about four hours. Test with a skewer. Turn out on to a rack to cool. Leave for twelve hours. Cover with melted jelly, then almond paste. Stand for forty-eight hours in a dry room. Ice smoothly with royal icing. Cover remainder of icing with wet muslin, and leave till next day. Beat up remainder of icing. Pipe a design round edge of cake, and G.R. on side. Decorate with remainder of icing, flags and other decorations.

¶ ROYAL ICING : Beat two and a half pounds of icing sugar with five egg whites and three dessertspoons of lemon juice till fluffy just before required.

ROYAL GINGERBREAD

Gingerbread has always been popular in ancient days. Sometimes it weighed one hundred and fifty pounds. It was always served as a gift of welcome at royal christenings, weddings and Royal feasts. Sometimes the mixture was baked in the form of animals, birds and people, which were often gilded—hence the expression 'The gilt has come off the gingerbread'. There are old-fashioned moulds made of carved wood kept in the Royal kitchen for shaping gingerbread. I have also seen some in the museum in York.

A VERY OLD RECIPE OF CHARLES THE SECOND DATE *c.* 1660

One portion of ye finest flour, twelve ounces of sugar pounded to a great fyness, two ounces of ye fynest synger of ye Orient, and ye yolkes of eight fresh and large egges.

The directions are rather difficult to follow, but are something like this when turned into modern English: work these ingredients on a pastry board or slab, and after having gathered the paste up to a solid mass separate it into four parts and roll to the thickness of the sixth of an inch, one after the other. Then with a cutter cut out as many cakes as the paste will produce and place them on a buttered baking sheet. Pass a paste brush over them when they are about half cooked. Shake over them some sugar and some carraway seeds, and set back again in oven to finish baking. When cooked, they should be of a light hue.

THIS RECIPE WAS USED IN THE ROYAL KITCHEN
1701

Take six pounds of flour, two ounces of ground ginger, two ounces of carraway seeds, and half a pound of powdered loaf sugar. Mix together with four pounds clarified treacle. Mix well till there is no flour to be seen. Then take one pound of fresh butter and work it in, and bake.

DUKE OF WINDSOR'S GINGERBREAD
c. 1920

Gingerbread has been a favourite cake of the Duke of Windsor ever since he was a little boy. His Aunt said he always asked for it to be made 'sweet and sticky'. This recipe is for a gingerbread that used to be made in the kitchens of St James's Palace and Buckingham Palace especially for His Royal Highness.

> 1 lb butter
> 2 lbs flour
> $\frac{1}{2}$ lb brown sugar
> 2 ozs powdered ginger
> 1 lb sweet almonds
> $1\frac{1}{2}$ ozs ground carraway seeds
> 4 ozs chopped candied peel
> 1 oz allspice
> $\frac{1}{2}$ teaspoon bicarbonate of soda
> 2 lbs treacle
> 6 eggs

Rub butter into the flour. Add the sugar, ginger, the almonds, blanched and chopped a little, carraway seeds, candied peel, allspice and soda. Mix well together. Beat the treacle and eggs well together. Stir into dry ingredients. Pour into two shallow buttered baking tins, filling them only half full, and bake about one and a half hours in a moderate oven.

ROYAL WEDDING CAKE *c.* 1760

1½ lbs butter
1½ lbs sifted sugar
2½ lbs sifted flour
1 oz salt
12 eggs
1 lb cleaned currants
½ pint brandy
¼ gill caramel or burnt sugar colouring
½ lb ground almonds
1 lb chopped dried cherries
1½ lbs shredded orange, lemon and
    green citron peel
The zest of 4 oranges
1 oz pounded cinnamon, cloves, nutmegs
    and coriander seeds in equal pro-
    portions

First work the butter in a large white pan with a wooden spoon until it presents the appearance of a creamy substance. Next add by degrees, the sugar, flour, salt and eggs, still continuing to work the batter the whole of the time. Then add the remainder of the ingredients and as soon as all is thoroughly incorporated, let the preparation be poured into a proper-sized tin hoop, previously lined with a double band of buttered paper, and ready placed upon a stout baking sheet, the bottom of which must also be lined with double sheet of paper. Bake in a moderate heat and be careful not to increase the heat of the oven while baking. A cake of this weight will require about four hours' baking.

¶ ICING FOR THE CAKE: when the cake is cold and

cleaned of paper, place on a baking sheet and cover the top
with a coating of orgeate paste, one inch and a half in thickness, and dry this in the oven for an hour. Then cover the
whole surface of the cake with royal icing about half an inch
in thickness and when this has become hard, decorate it with
royal icing piped on the top and sides in tasteful ornamental
design, using birds, buds and leaves of all kinds. Blush rose-
buds may be used in similitude of youthful blushes, but white
is essential.

I should think 'orgeate paste' is a variety of almond paste. E.C.

'TO MAKE A CAKE SUCH AS WE HAD FOR THE CHRISTENING OF MY YOUNG RELATIVE'

VICTORIA *c.* 1849

Take four quarts of very fine flour, four pounds of fresh
butter, two pounds of fine sugar, four pounds of cleaned currants, two pounds of stoned raisins, two dozen fresh eggs (or
six eggs to every quart of flour), half an ounce of ground
mace, half an ounce of grated nutmeg, a little citron. Bake for
about three hours. Then beat the whites of many eggs to a
froth, and to each egg, add five spoonfuls of the finest sugar
and beat it gradually in and for a great while. Put this on
when the cake is hot and set it in a warm oven to dry.

THE SAME CAKE BAKED BY THE BARONESS . . . .

Beat the butter to a cream. Pound the nutmeg and mace
finely. Wash the currants and raisins in several waters and
stone and chop the latter. Cut the citron into slices of an inch
in thickness and chop one pound of blanched almonds. Beat
the yolks of the eggs with the sugar to a smooth paste. Beat
the butter and the flour together, and add them to the yolks
and sugar. Then add the spices and cast in half a pint of the
finest brandy and the whites of the eggs already mentioned,
beaten to a stiff froth. Beat the whole mixture together, and
stir into it the currants, raisins, almonds and a pinch of salt.
Butter the cake pan and line with buttered paper. The cake

mixture should be about two and a half inches deep in the cake tin. Bake from three to four hours in a moderate oven.

ALMOND PASTE c. 1560

As made by Maids-of-Honour of Queen Elizabeth the First

Scald in boyling water and well soak good almonds for four hours. Then drain and pound them, adding thereto dropps of damask rosewater and when well beaten into a pulp rub through a hair sieve upon a platter. Add to the pulp an ounce of passed gum dragon, which is gum soaked in tepid river water, and passed through a cloth. Place the prepared gum upon a clean marble slab and work with the hands, until it appears white and flexible. Then add the almond pulp and half a pound of fine sugar and continue to work together until a fine paste is produced.

'Passed' means strained. E.C.

ICING FOR CAKES

AS USED FOR BIRTHDAY AND CHRISTMAS CAKES

Copied by Queen Victoria, Kensington Palace, 1835

Mix a pound of refined sugar, sifted very fine with the whites of twenty-four eggs, in an earthen pan. Whisk them very well for three or four hours, till whites are thick and white, and then with a thin broad knife or bunch of feathers, spread it all over the top and sides of the cake. Set the cake before a clear fire and keep it turning continually that it may not change colour. But better to place in a cool oven for an hour. This will harden it.

TO MAKE A GOOD CAKE c. 1709

Take four quarts of fine flour, two and a half pounds of butter, three-quarters of a pound of sugar, one pound of almonds finely beaten, half a pint of sack, one pint of good ale yeast, one pint of boiling cream, twelve yolks, four whites of eggs, and four pounds of currants. When you have wrought this into a fine paste, let it be kept warm by the fire half an hour before you set it in the oven. If you please, you may put into it two pounds of raisins of the sun, stoned and quartered.

¶ THE ICE FOR THE CAKE: take the white of three new-laid eggs, and three-quarters of a pound of fine sugar finely beaten with the whites of the eggs, and ice the cake. Let your oven be of a temperate heat, then let your cake stand overnight before you ice it, and afterwards only to harden the ice.

QUEEN ALEXANDRA ICING c. 1903

¼ lb unsalted butter
3 ozs sifted icing sugar
Colouring and flavouring to taste

Beat butter until softened, then gradually beat in sugar. Beat until creamy and smooth. Stir in coffee essence or extract, or melted chocolate to taste, or flavour with rose water and colour with cochineal, or add a drop or two of almond essence and colour with sap green. Use with sponge and very plain cakes, for this icing is very rich.

BEVERAGES, WINES
AND CORDIALS

YOU have to go a long way back to become familiar with the beverages with which kings and queens and their courtiers slaked their thirst in ancient days. The Saxons, it is claimed, introduced brewing to England, and ale or *alu*, as it was then called, was the beverage served at coronations long before the Roman Conquest. It was also one of the beverages provided at the royal banquets of Edward the Confessor about 1042. In the days of Henry the Eighth, breakfast for three consisted of a chine of beef, a manchet (a loaf of fine wheat bread) and a gallon of ale.

Queen Elizabeth, who served beer at all royal functions, was fond of it herself. Ale, of course, was the national beverage in mediæval days, as it still is. It is said that when the queen made her State visits, barrels of the very strong beer she favoured had to be procured before her arrival. Leicester is often quoted as writing that the Virgin Queen's taste was said to be for a beer 'so strong as there was no man able to drink it'. It was in Elizabeth's reign that a current saying ran: 'The Spaniard eats, the German drinks, and the English exceed in both.'

The lovely, ill-fated Mary, Queen of Scots, was also a beer drinker. History relates that when Her Majesty was confined at Walsingham her secretary is reported to have asked 'At what place near Tulbury Castle may good beer be purchased for Her Majesty?' This is a surprise to me. I should have thought that with her long connection with France the inquiry would have been about claret.

Mead, which was also very popular in this period, did not survive like ale, but it has come into its own again of late years, not only as a beverage, but in flavouring dishes. Morat, made from mulberries, seems to have lost favour, while cider has gained in prestige.

Queen Victoria, by transcribing her favourite receipts in her 'Scrap Books', shows that many of the beverages which were famous several generations ago were still popular in Victorian days. Some, particularly the cordials, are still in vogue.

A CLARET DRINK c. 1842

Mix a bottle of claret and a bottle of soda water together. Add a small glass of brandy, sugar to taste and a lump of ice.

A CORDIAL c. 1805

Two quarts of spring water, one quart of brandy, six Lisbon lemons, half a pound of fine sugar.

A DELICIOUS SUMMER DRINK c. 1855

Take two washed and dried lemons, one and three-quarter pounds of powdered loaf sugar, one quart of white wine, and three quarts of quite fresh boiling milk. Peel the lemons very thinly. Squeeze the juice over peel, and let it soak in juice all night. Next morning, add the sugar, the wine and the boiling milk. Strain through a jelly bag till quite clear, then set on ice.

'A DRINK I LIKE'

Victoria, February 1836

Boil a quart of spring water. Add to it a yolk of one egg, the juice of a single lemon, nine large spoonfuls of sweet white wine, with sugar to taste, and of syrup of lemons one ounce.

A GOOD DRINK OF TEA *c.* 1708

Dated 'Queen Anne'

Make a quart of very excellently brewed tea. Pour it out and set it over the fire, and beat therein the yolkes of four eggs, and a pint of white wine, a grated nutmeg, and sugar to taste. Stirr over fire till very hot. Drink in china dishes.

A POSSET OF ALE *c.* 1728

1 bottle strong ale
Sugar to taste
Grated nutmeg to taste
1 pint new milk
1 tablespoon fine sieved breadcrumbs

Pour ale into a bowl. Sweeten to taste. Season with grated nutmeg. Stir occasionally until sugar is dissolved. Pour milk into a saucepan. Add crumbs. Stir until boiling. Pour into the ale, stirring constantly. Leave until the 'head' rises, then serve.

AN OLD RECEIPT
FOR BARLEY WATER *c.* 1690

Wash an ounce of barley (pearl), shift it twice, put to it three pints of water, an ounce of sweet almonds, blanched and beaten finely, and some lemon peel. Boil till you have a smooth liquor, and put therein some sirop of lemons and sirop of orange flowers. A sure cure for the cold if served hot.

CHERRY BRANDY *c.* 1841

Put three pounds of Morella cherries, freshly gathered and with half of their stalks removed, into a glass bottle, strewing in between them the finest loaf sugar, one pound and two ounces in all. If wanted very sweet, add another four ounces. When bottle is almost full, pour in one and a half pints of good brandy, and add three or four blanched bitter almonds. Cork up bottle. Tie over a piece of bladder, and store away in a dry place for three months. Filter through blotting paper and pour into a fresh bottle and seal. Can be used in two months.

CHERRY SYRUP *c.* 1843

Make one pound of sugar with half a pint of water into a syrup of thirty-two degrees of strength. Pound together half a pound of red currants and enough Kentish cherries to give you a pint of juice when strained. Mix the juice slowly with the syrup. Bottle and seal.

COWSLIP WINE *c.* 1852

To twelve gallons of water, add twenty-eight pounds of fine, Lisbon sugar. Place in a copper with the stiffly-frothed whites of six eggs. Keep stirring till the mixture boils when skim well and leave till just blood warm. Then add nineteen quarts of cowslips, the strained juice and washed rinds of six lemons, and half a pint of yeast. Let this work for four or five days, then add two quarts of brandy, and put in prepared cask. When yeast stops working, cork up cask. Fit for bottling when fine.

CURRANT SHRUB *c.* 1860

Squeeze the currants through a coarse cloth. Take two quarts of the juice, one gallon of rum, and fourteen ounces of double refined sugar. Mix the juice, rum and sugar together, then strain through a flannel bag, as you would jelly, but don't squeeze it.

CURRANT WINE (i) *c.* 1845

Gather the currants when fully ripe. Mash and squeeze them through a clean cloth, throwing the pulp into a pan of water. To one quart of juice, put two quarts of the water in which the pulp was, then add three and a quarter pounds of sugar to every gallon of liquor. Let this stand a day and a night, then turn it into a cask after rinsing it out with a little brandy. If liked, add a gallon of raspberries to about eight gallons of water.

CURRANT WINE (ii) *c.* 1850

To every gallon of bruised currants, stalks and all, put a gallon and a half of water, letting it stand three or four hours. Then strain through cheese cloth and add three pounds of best loaf sugar to every gallon of liquor. When the sugar is dissolved, put liquor into a clean dry cask, but don't stop it up until fermentation has ceased.

DAMSON BRANDY *c.* 1843

Pick your damsons, wipe them, then fill a bottle three-quarters full with the fruit, and pour in the brandy. Add sugar to taste. The brandy should not entirely fill the bottle so as to leave room for the swelling of the fruit. Cork bottle tightly, and shake bottle twice or thrice a week for three months when it is ready for use. Strain through blotting paper into another bottle.

GINGER WINE (i) *c.* 1747

Ten gallons of water, ten pounds of lump sugar and two ounces of ginger, bruised. Boil together, scum it, and put the whites of eight eggs, well beaten together, to clarify it. Scum it all the time it boils then remove from fire and strain it into a vessel, adding the peels and juice of as many lemons as you have gallons of liquor. Put half a spoon of yeast on top and stop the cask closely. In a fortnight the wine will be fit to bottle, and in another fortnight to drink. The lemons must be peeled very thinly and the juice strained before it is added to the liquor.

GINGER WINE (ii) *c.* 1732

Allow twenty-two pounds of moist sugar to nine gallons of water, also eighteen lemons and six ounces of ginger. Take off the rind of the lemons as thin as possible, bruise the ginger, and boil it with the lemon peel and sugar, and a little water taken from the nine gallons for half an hour. Now chop four pounds of raisins and put into the cask with the juice of the lemons, pulp and seeds. Pour the boiling syrup over them. When cool, add two spoonfuls of good barm. Let this remain for a week, stirring it every day, then add at least a pint of brandy and one ounce of isinglass. When the fermentation stops, cork up the cask. The wine may be bottled in six or eight weeks. To boil with the syrup the whites of one or two eggs, well beaten, will greatly assist in making the wine clear.

HOTTE MILK OF ALMONDES *c.* 1510

A FAVOURITE OF QUEEN ANNE BOLEYN

To make hotte mylk of almondes, take blanched almondes and grind them, and draw them with faire water, with sugar or clarified honey, then salt it and boile it, and serve it fairlie hot with toasted bred therein.

IMPERIAL WATER

Copied in Queen Victoria's handwriting, and dated
Kensington Palace, 1836

Called after Napoleon Bonaparte: put into a large jug, two ounces of cream of tartar with the strained juice and grated peel of six lemons. Pour on seven quarts of boiling spring water. When cold, clear it through a gauze sieve. Sweeten and bottle it up until the next day when it may be used.

GEORGE THE FOURTH'S RUM DRINK
c. 1825

Peel of 2 Seville oranges
Peel of 12 lemons
2 quarts of rum
2 quarts of cold spring water
1 lb loaf sugar
1 pint strong green tea
¼ pint maraschino
1 pint lemon juice
1 pint Madeira
1 grated nutmeg
1 pint boiling milk

Infuse the peels of the oranges and lemons in the rum for twelve hours. Add to water loaf sugar, green tea, maraschino, lemon juice, Madeira and nutmeg. Mix all together and stir in boiling milk last. Let stand for six hours, then strain through a jelly bag till quite clear, and bottle for use.

KING GEORGE THE FIFTH'S FAVOURITE BARLEY WATER RECEIPT
c. 1922

The King used to drink this every day at lunch. I hear it was even specially made for him when he lunched in Belfast on his visit to Ireland.

4 large tablespoons of barley
2 ozs fine sugar
½ lemon
2 pints boiling water

Wash the barley very well, and put into a well heated jug. Add the sugar and strained lemon juice, and rind, peeled carefully so as to avoid taking with it any of the tough and bitter coating of the fruit. Pour in the boiling water. Cover and leave till cold. Ice an improvement.

This drink is sometimes made with soda water, when the recipe is three teaspoonfuls of lemon juice, two teaspoonfuls of sugar, half a glass of barley water, and half a glass of soda water. Mix the lemon juice and sugar together in a tumbler, half fill with barley water, and then add the soda water. Drink whilst effervescing.

NOTE: 'This drink was often mixed on the sideboard for George the Fifth by one of his carvers.'

LEMON BRANDY

'This is a drink much liked by King William and Queen Adelaide.' VICTORIA. *June 2nd, 1835*

Take ten lemons, pare very thinn, steep all the carnels [pips] in one gallon of good brandy, closely covered, for three days. Then take three pints or three quarts of river water, and boyle it with two pounds of refined sugar, skim it, then squeeze in the juice of eight lemons, then put it to ye brandy, and stirre well together and straine through a jelly sack [bag] and boyle.

MAY BLOSSOM CORDIAL *c.* 1775

Try to choose the may blossom [hawthorn] on a dry still day when there is no dust blowing. Gather as many full-blown flowers as will fill a large wide-necked bottle. Fill up with brandy. Cork securely, and stand for three months, shaking bottle three times a week, for three months. Strain through blotting paper into another bottle, and use as a flavouring for custards and sweet sauces.

MILK PUNCH *c.* 1832

Take eighteen lemons, wipe and peel off rind very thinly, then steep it for three days in one quart of rum or shrub.

Afterwards add three quarts of rum, five quarts of water, the juice of the eighteen lemons, strained, three pounds of loaf sugar, and two quarts of fresh boiling milk. Cover closely and leave for several hours when strain through a jelly bag and bottle for use. To make milk punch from oranges, use eighteen oranges, but add the strained juice of three or four lemons as well.

PRINCESS MARY COCKTAIL *c.* 1921

Mix in a cocktail shaker one-third each of dry gin and Crème de Cacao. Add a little cracked ice. Shake well. Pour out, and float a third of thick cream gently on top.

RED POPPY CORDIAL *c.* 1840

'*Swift Water*'. VICTORIA

Take three red poppies that grow among the corn and put them into one gallon of brandy. Steep two days and nights and then wring them out and put the water [I suppose the writer means the liquor] into a glass then put to it one pound of fine sugar, two pounds of raisins of the sun, stoned, two ounces of the best liquorish, scraped and sliced, one ounce of bruised anniseed, one ounce of Venice treacle, half an ounce of saffron, dried and rubbed, one pint of cowslip water, a quarter ounce of long pepper, bruised, a quarter ounce of Virginia snake root, and a quarter ounce of cardamons. Put them all together in the glass and sett in the sun for three weeks. Shake it once a day then strain it for use.

ROYAL HIPOCRAS CUP *c.* 1659

IPOCRAS

The wines of olden times were somewhat different from the wines of today. Rumney, Ossey, Malmesey, Sack and Hypocras were then in great favour. This is the recipe for the Hypocras Cup which was served at the Coronation banquets of Henry the Seventh, Henry the Eighth, Anne Boleyn, Queen

E*

Elizabeth the First, James the First, Queen Anne, and doubt-
less many other sovereigns of England.
Mix a gallon of Hypocras with four pounds of cinnamon, two
pounds of ginger, one ounce of cloves, eleven pounds of sugar,
eleven pounds of small raisins and eleven pounds of dates.

NOYEAU c. 1888

Put four ounces bitter almonds, blanched and beaten to a
paste, into a quart of English gin. Keep bottle in a moderate
heat for a week, shaking it often. Then dip a pound of sugar
into cold water, and place in a basin till it dissolves, then add
it to the gin and leave for twenty-four hours, shaking it often.
Filter through blotting paper and bottle for use.

SYRUP OF ROSES c. 1815

*'As made for Her Royal Highness, Princess Charlotte,
the daughter of George the Fourth.'* VICTORIA

Gather one pound of damask rose leaves with the dew still
upon their leaves, and scarcely open to the morning sun, and
therefore very fragrant. Put them in an earthen vessel, add a
quart of boiling spring water, and cover the vessel closely.
Let this remain for six hours, not more nor less, then run the
liquor through a piece of fine muslin cloth, and add to it a
pint of the juice of the roses, a pound and a half of loaf sugar,
then boil over a brisk fire till a good syrup be made, only be
careful in the skimming and do not boil for over long—just
until the syrup is formed. Then preserve in bottles closely
corked. A couple of eggs can be added to clear if desired.

SACK WHEY c. 1681

1 pint milk
2 glasses white wine
Sugar to taste

Bring milk to boyling point. Add wine. Heat till the mixture comes to the boyle. Draw pan to side of stove. Leave till the curd settles, then strain off whey. Sweeten to taste. A refreshing drink for invalids.

SHRUB *c.* 1892

Take one gallon and a pint of brandy, one quart of lemon and orange juice, two pounds of the finest loaf sugar, the peel of six oranges, and six ditto [presumably lemons are meant]. Steep them twenty-four hours in some of the brandy. Strain off the lemon and orange juice, then put all together in the cask or bottle, shaking it twice a day, for a fortnight, then let it settle and bottle it off. When you wish to drink the punch, allow half a pint of water to a quarter pint of the Shrub.

SLOE WINE *c.* 1897

Boil an equal quantity of fruit and water for fifteen minutes, then strain it off and for every gallon of liquor, allow four pounds of best loaf sugar. Boil all up together and skim it then put in a tub, and when cool, put in a toast spread over with yeast. Let it work two or three days, then barrel it. If it is intended for old wine, there must be an extra half pound of sugar allowed for every gallon.

TO MAKE ALE *c.* 1879

Take three pounds of loaf sugar, and five gallons of water with enough of essence of spruce to give it a flavour, a cup of good yeast, some lemon peel, and when fermented bottle it up closely.

TO MAKE SILLYBUBBLES *c.* 1510

*As made for Queen Anne Boleyn, Queen Consort
of Henry the Eighth*

Take a quart of cream and half a pound of fine sugar, a pint of good red wine, a half a pint of strong ale. Whip it, and when it froths, save some of the froth on a sieve to top them. Then fill the glasses half full with that when it is not whipt much, and then fill it up with the whip and top them with that which is on the sieve.

TO MULL WINE *c.* 1861

In Queen Victoria's handwriting

Boil some spice in a little water till the flavour be gained. Then add an equal quantity of good port wine, some sugar and nutmeg. Boil, and serve with crisp unsweetened biscuits.

WINE WHEY *c.* 1840

Place half a pint of new milk upon the fire, and when it boils, pour into it as much sour white wine as will completely 'turn' it, and it looks clear. Let it boil up. Then set the saucepan aside till the curd subsides and do not stir it. Pour the whey off and add to it half a pint of boiling water, and some white sugar. So will be produced a whey clear of milk particles.

SIR WALTER RALEIGH'S CORDIAL WATER 1654

Put a gallon of strawberries into a pint of *aqua vitae*. Let them remain for four or five days. Strain them gently. Sweeten the water to taste with fine sugar and perfume to taste.

WHITE DRINK *c.* 1679

One gallon of honey, and four gallons of water. Boyle together till scum be boyled off. Put in spice, a little cinnamon, ginger, mace and cloves. Boyle with spice in it till it is so thick it can beat an egg. Then take from fire and allow to cool in a wooden vessel till it be lukewarm. Then put into it a hot toste of white bread after spreading on both sides of it thick barm that will presently make it work. Let it work for twelve hours, closely covered, then turn it into a runlet. Then putt in it lemon peel, keep a secret vessel for ten days, and then bottle. Drink in four months, not sooner. It is better after twelve months for it will then be quick, puissant, pure white and spritely.

I wonder if this is a species of Mead. E.C.

PRESERVES

When you turn the pages of ancient manuscript cook books, you are surprised at the trouble that was taken in Royal still-rooms to keep the Royal tables supplied with delicious preserves. Rose petals were turned into conserves, angelica and lettuce stalks were candied, and damsons were made into 'cheese'. Quinces were turned into honey, and apricots, green-gages and many other fruits were made into pastilles. In those days, 'the ladyes of high degree' took great pride in their preserves.

CRYSTALLIZED FRUITS *c.* 1772

> Fruit as required
> Whites of 2 eggs
> ¼ pint spring water
> 1 lb clear sugar

Currants, cherries, grapes, plums and raspberries, as well as many other fruits, can all be crystallized in this way: see first that the fruit is very perfect. Well beat the whites of the eggs, and mix them with the spring water. Dip fruits separately into the egg and water mixture, then roll them in the pounded sugar. Roll them several times, then turn them out on white paper to dry till they become crystallized. Arrange on a dish in green leaves when serving.

GRAND AUNT'S QUINCE CAKES *c.* 1780

Boyle some quinces slowly in water till softe. Rub through a hair sieve, then measure. To each cuppe of quince measure 1 cuppe of sugar. Putt quince pulpe and sugar in a basine. Beat together with a spoon till quite thick and ye colour of snow. Place in paper cases. Dry in a cool stove. Apricocks and greenegages can be made into cakes in ye same waye.

ORANGE MOONS *c.* 1651

Take several oranges and their weight in sugar. Boil oranges till their bitterness is gone, then take out the pips and the juice. Beat the peel very finely in a mortar, and add their equal weight in sugar. When mixed to a paste spread them thinly in dishes and set them fore a fire to dry, and then, when dried, store in a tin with paper between. Turn them from one side to the other while drying, and when stored, see that no air gets into them.

RASPBERRY PASTE

Copied by Queen Victoria from an old receipt, and dated, Kensington, 1835

Bruise a quart of ripe raspberries, and strain one half and put the juice obtained to the other half, and boil for fifteen minutes. Add a pint of red currant juice and boil together till raspberries are cooked. Then put one and a half pounds of refined sugar into a clean pan with as much spring water as will dissolve it, and boil it to a sugar again. Then add the raspberries and the juice, give them a scalding, and pour into glasses or plates. Put them on to dry on stone. Turn them, when necessary, and store away for use.

RASPBERRY PASTILLES

Copied by Queen Victoria, and dated, Kensington, 1835

'Put half a pound of pounded loaf sugar upon a flat dish, squeeze the juice of raspberries through a sieve on to the sugar till a paste is made. Drop upon paper and put in oven to dry. Currant pastils can be made in the same way.'

TO KEEP GOOSEBERRIES OR GRAPES ALL THE WINTER *c.* 1860

Have these fruits when at the full growth, but not ripe, and put them in close bottles, and cork them close, and tie them over with leather, that no air can get into them; then set them in a cold cellar, and keep them for your own use. So you may keep cherries or damsons.

APPLE JELLY *c.* 1880

Weigh out twelve pounds of apples after peeling and coring them. Cut them in slices and put in a large preserving pan along with just as much water as will keep them from burning. Cook till tender, then strain through a jelly bag and to every quart of juice, add three-quarter pound of sugar. Boil till stiff enough to pot.

CHERRY JAM *c.* 1882

Stone cherries, remove the kernels, and blanch them, and add to the fruit. Then allow to every pound of cherries, a pound of sugar. Boil all together for three-quarters of an hour and pot as usual.

CURRANT CHEESE *c.* 1879

When you make currant jelly, and have taken away the clear jelly from it, take the thick part for your currant cheese. To a pint of the thick, allow a quarter pound of coarse sugar and let this boil till very thick. It requires to boil a good while before it sets. The most successful way I have found is to boil the currant pulp for a little before adding the sugar.

EARLY VICTORIAN DAMSON CHEESE
c. 1841

Wash the damsons in a colander under the cold water tap. Drain well, and place in a saucepan. Heat slowly at the back of your stove till the juice flows, then rub them through a sieve that retains the seeds, into another pan. To each three pints of juice, add two pounds of loaf sugar. Stir together till sugar is dissolved, then bring to the boil. Boil, stirring frequently, till a little sets stiff when tested on a cold plate. Pot and seal. Serve as a preserve at tea or with milk moulds.

PLUM MARMALADE c. 1867

Weigh very ripe plums after wiping and stoning them, and then measure out equal quantity of sugar. Put fruit into preserving pan after passing it through a sieve, and stir constantly. At first it will thin and then as the juice steams off it will thicken. When you think it has got so dry that it may burn any moment, stir sugar well in, and keep on stirring till the surface of the mixture shivers before bursting into bubbles. Then it is ready so remove from fire and pot at once. You must never stop stirring from the time you put the fruit in the pan.

ROSE PETAL JAM c. 1713

20 sweet-scented roses
3 lbs loaf sugar
2 pints water
$\frac{1}{2}$ teaspoon citric acid

Use cabbage roses if available, otherwise red, strongly-scented roses, or a mixture of red and pink. Gather when fully open but still fresh. Dissolve sugar in the water. Stir till boiling.

Boil for half an hour. Remove all white heels from roses and pull petals to pieces. Place in a basin. Cover with half a pint of boiling water. Soak until thoroughly moistened, then pour soaking water and petals into boiling syrup, stirring constantly. When boiling, boil for half an hour, stirring frequently with a silver or wooden spoon, and pressing the petals down frequently in the syrup, as some will float on the top. When tender and clear, add citric acid. Boil from ten to fifteen minutes to setting point. Pot and seal.

POTTED BIRDS *c.* 1840

Clean the pigeons or any other small birds, and season them inside and out with salt, ground allspice and ground pepper. Rub every part well with seasoning, then lay, breast downwards, in a pan. Pack the birds as closely as you can. Spread thickly with butter. Cover with a wet paste of flour and water, then cover with a buttered paper. Bake in an oven till birds are tender in about an hour. When cold, remove paste. Cut into joints for serving and pack closely into potting pots which somewhat resemble casseroles. Try to allow no space between the joints. Cover deeply with melted butter. The butter that has been used for covering potted birds can be used for basting or for paste for meat pies.

PRINCE OF WALES CATSUP *c.* 1890

> 1 pint elderberry vinegar
> 2 ozs anchovies
> 1 oz shallots
> 1 teaspoon whole cloves
> 1 teaspoon ground mace
> 1 teaspoon ground ginger
> 1 teaspoon grated nutmeg

To prepare elderberry vinegar, strip ripe berries from the stalks. Place in a fireproof jar. Fill up with vinegar. Place in a cool oven, then stand overnight. Strain through a jelly bag into an enamel saucepan. Add anchovies. Peel and slice in shallots. Add spices. Bring to boil. Simmer gently till the anchovies are dissolved. Leave until cold. Strain and bottle. Cork tightly.

TO PICKLE WALNUTS *c.* 1852

Take green walnuts before the shell is grown to any hardness in them, pick them from the stalks, and put them into cold water, and set them on a gentle fire till the outward skin begins to peel off. Then put them into a tub or pot, and add water and salt to them, changing once a day for ten or twelve days, till the bitterness and discolouring of the water be gone. Then take a good quantity of mustard seed and beat it with vinegar till it becomes coarse mustard; some cloves of garlic and ginger; make a hole in each nut, and put in a little of this. Then take white wine (and white wine vinegar) and boyle it together; and as you are going to take it off the fire, put in pepper, ginger, cloves and some of the mustard and garlic, according to your discretion. Then cover the kettle till they are cold, then put them into a jar, bottle or well-glazed pot, and keep them under the liquid, close tight down with leather for your use.

STRAWBERRIES

*In Queen Victoria's own handwriting,
dated Kensington Palace,* 1836

Gather on a fine and sunny day, so that the fruit may be dry, some fine scarlet strawberries. Lay them with care separately upon a deep china dish. Beat and sift over them twice their weight of double refined sugar. Take then a few ripe strawberries and put them in a jar with their weight of double refined sugar, and cover closely. Let them stand in a kettle of boiling water till soft and the syrup is out of them. Strain them then through a muslin cloth into a tossing pan, and boil and skim well. When cold, put in the whole strawberries and set over the fire till syrup be warm. Then take them off the fire and stand till quite cold. Set them then again upon the fire and make them a little hotter, and do so several times until they be quite clear. But do not permit that they boil or the stalks will come off when cold. Put into jelly glasses, with the stalks downwards. Fill up with the syrup and tie down closely.

This sounds like a preserve of unhulled strawberrries, a form of Bar-le-Duc. *I should put berries in a double boiler, with water in pan below.* E.C.

MISCELLANEOUS

BLACK HOG'S PUDDING *c.* 1840

BOIL a quartern of oatmeal very tender either in beef broth or in the broth that a pluck of a pig has been boiled in. Cover it well with liquor, season with quarter ounce of Jamaica pepper, finely pounded, and the same quantity of ground black pepper. Add a good handful of salt, the crumbs of a penny loaf, grated, five eggs, well beaten, a little thyme, two large handfuls of penny royal, a good quantity of cleaned leeks, a large peeled onion, a little sage and rosemary, four or five tops of young fennel, and the same quantity of lavender heads. Chop all the herbs very small with a small quantity of spinach, and mix with the other ingredients. Add as much blood of the pig as will colour the mixture well, cut into small pieces a good piece of the fat of your leaf—about six pounds. Mix all well together in a deep large vessel, except the fat which lay by itself for your greater certainty of regularly disposing of it. Fill all the guts not too full for fear of bursting them. Put into boiling water. When it boils too fast, sprinkle a little cold water round them, and press constantly down with a smooth stick or thievil [porridge stick]. Boil them an hour and a quarter.

WHITE HOG'S PUDDING *c.* 1820

Quarter pound of Jordan almonds, blanched and beat fine in a mortar with a little sprinkling of rose water to keep them from oiling, quarter pound of grated Naples biscuits, a pint of cream, two and a quarter pounds of rice flour, boiled in it till it is thick, one pound of cleaned currants, sixteen eggs, leaving out the whites of eight, the marrow of two beef bones cut small, half a pound of beef suet, shredded small, the crumbs of a penny loaf, soaked in boiling milk, sugar, salt, grated nutmeg, and orange flower water to taste. Mix and fill the small guts. Boil for three-quarters of an hour. If too stiff, add a little more cream to mixture before filling guts.

PORRIDGE *c.* 1832

Take three-quarters of a pint of fresh milk and boil with four ounces of fresh butter in a large saucepan, then stir quickly into it six ounces of oatmeal, wheatmeal or Indian maize. Continue to stir in the same way until the mixture adheres to the sides of the saucepan, which ought to be earthenware. Season before taking from the fire with chopped parsley and salt, or, if sweetness be preferred, with sugar and cinnamon.

PRINCESS LOUISE'S SCRAMBLED EGGS
c. 1879

$\frac{1}{2}$ pint green asparagus tips
2 ozs butter
5 fresh eggs
1 tablespoon cream
Salt and pepper to taste
Grating of nutmeg

Cut off only the points of the asparagus tips. They should not be more than three-quarters of an inch long. (Use the remainder of the stalks for soup.) Place them carefully in a shallow saucepan. Cover with boiling, salted water. Bring to boil. Boil, uncovered, until tender. Drain thoroughly. Melt half the butter in a small shallow saucepan. Toss tips in the butter over low heat for about two minutes. Meanwhile, break eggs into a basin. Add cream and seasonings. Beat well. Melt butter in a small saucepan. Add egg mixture.

Stir over moderate heat for a minute or so until eggs show signs of thickening, then pour in cooked tips. Stir till mixture starts to set. Dish up. Garnish with sippets of thin toast and minced parsley.

DESERT ISLAND *c.* 1600

Copied by Queen Victoria and dated, Kensington Palace, 1835

Make a lump of paste into a rock three inches broad at the top. Colour it to taste and put it in the centre of a deep china dish. Get [set] a cast figure on it with a crown on the head and a knot of rock candy at the feet. Then make a roll of paste an inch thick. Stick it on the inner edge of the dish, all the way round. Cut eight pieces of eringo root, about three inches long, and fix them upright upon the roll of paste on the edge. Make gravel walks of comfits round the dish. Set small figures in them and roll out the paste. Cut it open like Chinese rails and bake it. Fit it on either side of the gravel walks with gum. Form an entrance where the rails are with two pieces of eringo roots for pillars.

I think eringo must mean angelica. E.C.

VINEGARS

¶ CUCUMBER VINEGAR: Pare and slice fifteen large cucumbers. Put them in a stone jar with three pints of vinegar, four large onions, sliced, two or three shallots, a little garlic, two large spoonfuls of salt, three teaspoons of pepper and half a teaspoon of cayenne pepper. After standing for four days, give the whole a boil. When cold, strain and filter the liquor through paper. Keep in small bottles to add to salad, or eat with cold meat. *c.* 1850.

¶ CURRANT VINEGAR: Mash twelve gallons ripe white currants in twenty-four gallons cold water, then stand for four days when strain through cheese cloth, or squeeze through a hair sieve. Boil half of the liquor and mix together. Add a pound of the coarsest sugar to every gallon of liquor.

Allow to stand in a dry place for six months when it will be ready for use. *c.* 1857.

¶ GOOSEBERRY VINEGAR: To every gallon of fully ripe gooseberries measure off two gallons of cold water that has been boiled. Bruise berries well with your hands, then stir into the water. Stand for three days, stirring well once a day, then squeeze all the juice through a jelly bag into a large vessel and to every gallon of the gooseberry water, add one pound of coarse sugar. Place a paper over to keep dust out, and stand for a month or two when drain it off. Clean off the lees with a little vinegar, then pour back the gooseberry vinegar, and allow to stand anywhere within doors for six to twelve months till fine and sharp enough. The longer the better. When fine, bottle it off. *c.* 1860.

VERJUS 1849

(VERJUICE)

This is the name given to the sour juice of crab apples or grapes. It is used more in France than in England to destroy the 'flatness' of certain dishes. Where lemon juice or vinegar is usually added in England, to sharpen the flavour, verjuice is usually added in France.

¶ TO PREPARE VERJUICE FROM CRAB APPLES: Choose and stalk ripe apples, pile them up in a heap, and leave them to sweat. Keep removing any rotten patches, then mash fruit and strain off juice. Leave to ferment for one month, then bottle.

ADVICE TO A CARVER

'A carver should be a person of equable temper, pleasing and civil, scrupulous as to the care of his person. In appearance he should be grave and dignified, not given to unpleasant habits, such as yawning, sneezing, twisting his mouth, or scratching his head. He ought to be able to divide the viands to suit the taste of all present.' In early times the carving was done at Royal feasts by the most distinguished male person present, the King, of course, excluded. But in later years a 'Kerver' was appointed, and the above rules were laid down as to his person besides rules relating to carving.

ROYAL CHRISTMAS FARE

CHRISTMAS in England, in mediæval times, was a great Church festival, celebrated almost exclusively by the King and his barons. It was not until much later that all classes took part in its observance.

During the reigns of Henry the Eighth and Edward the Sixth, the annual feast was celebrated with great pomp. Edward's sister, Queen Mary, in her brief reign, robbed it of much of its splendour, but Queen Elizabeth the First, who loved to preserve the old customs, soon revived its ancient glory. One reads of magnificent celebrations conducted by Lord Robert Dudley, afterwards Earl of Leicester, at the Inner Temple in the fourth year of her reign. Towards the end of the Elizabethan period, when the Queen was worried with affairs of State, Christmas was more quietly celebrated. James the First soon restored its splendour, and Charles the First also made it a memorable feast. In both reigns, the performance of plays and masques were the principal items in the programmes. Ben Jonson for several years held the position of masque writer to the Court of King James.

There is a great difference between the Royal fare of today and the Royal fare of mediæval days. In mediæval days, the

Boar's Head crowned the feast. It was carried to the board on a silver dish, heralded with a flourish of trumpets, followed by a procession singing the ancient carol:

> *The Boar's Head in hand bring I*
> *With garlands gay and rosemary,*
> *I pray you all sing merrily.*

James the First, who disliked Boar's Head, is credited with substituting turkey for it at Christmas feasts.

The Royal Christmas fare of today has partly developed from the old-time fare. Yesterday crudely roasted thighs of deer kept Hotte Peacocke and Swan's Pie company at Royal Christmas dinners; in the days of Charles the First, five swans were sometimes roasted for the Royal Christmas dinner. To-day roast goose or turkey reign king of the feast, and a sirloin of beef is often in attendance. Plum pudding, which is now queen of the feast, is a royal descendant of Plum Broth, by way of Plum Pottage and Plum Porridge. It was not until the days of William and Mary that the original Plum Broth, which was served as soup in the days of Charles the First, and was composed of mutton stock, currants, prunes, raisins, sack and sherry, and later on was stiffened with brown bread, became known as a Plum Pudding.

In early days, no Christmas feast was complete without a most curious selection of pies, some filled with larks' tongues, some filled with seagull meat, some with lamprey and some with snails. These pies were originally made in an oval shape to represent the cradle in which the Holy Child was laid. During the feast, large flagons of spiced ale, called 'Lamb's Wool' were passed round. At the end of the feast, the Wassail Bowl was served, filled with hot, sweetened ale, cooked with roasted crabapples and toast. The bowl was usually decorated with ribbons.

TO PREPARE A BOAR'S HEAD
FOR CHRISTMAS *c.* 1880

As wild boars are practically beasts of the past, it is the domestic pig's head which, decorated in the most flamboyant

way, usually adorns the cold buffet on Christmas Day. Procure
a pig's head, specially cut, with a large piece of the neck
attached. Singe the head well. Wipe it very carefully with a
cloth, then scrape all over with a knife without scratching the
skin. If you want the head to present the appearance of a
boar's, see that the head is cut off before the pig is scalded
and the bristles singed off. Then lay on a cloth upon its face,
open it with a knife from the point of the under-jaw to the
cut part of the neck, and strip off the flesh clean from its
bones, without piercing the skin. Remove bones of the neck
in the same way, and cut flesh into long strips, two inches
thick and two inches broad. Now place head and strips of
flesh in a huge crock and rub well with half a pound of moist
brown sugar, a quarter pound of saltpetre, half an ounce dried
juniper berries, one teaspoonful cloves, two cloves of garlic,
five pounds of coarse kitchen salt. Then add to pickle four bay
leaves, four laurel leaves, a handful of thyme, a small pinch
of sage, basil, marjoram and lavender, and six blades of mace.
Turn head in this pickle every day for a week, keeping it in
a cool place meanwhile. When about to dress head, remove
from brine, wash it well with cold water, wipe it dry with a
clean cloth, then pare off all uneven parts, and line head with
the following forcemeat: one and a half pounds of veal and
half a pound each of fat bacon and sausage meat, all chopped
into mince, and mixed with a teaspoonful each of salt and
black pepper, two tablespoonfuls of parsley, finely chopped, a
pinch of ground mace and a handful of peeled, chopped mushrooms. These make a delicious forcemeat if all is first
pounded in a mortar, and moistened with the yolks of four
eggs.

TO STUFF A BOAR'S HEAD

Make forcemeat lining an inch in thickness, and arrange on
it regularly, fillets of tongue, bacon, truffles, and blanched
pistachio nuts. Cover garnish with another layer of the forcemeat, then repeat the garnish until the head is nicely filled
with stuffing to bring it up to its original size and shape. Now
sew up carefully to make sure no stuffing will escape. Wrap
in a clean linen cloth, and sew firmly into cloth, then place in

a braising pan. Cover with any carcase of game, preferably grouse, as its flavour is congenial to boar. Any trimmings of red meat will do. Moisten with wine *mirepoix* to cover the head. Boil up, skim thoroughly, then allow to simmer gently for five or six hours.

Remove and drain head and place upon a dish. If it has shrunk much, tighten cloth carefully to preserve shape, and return head to liquor. When cool and set, put head in a deep baking dish. Place in oven for a moment or two to melt the jelly that may be sticking to the cloth. Remove quickly, take off cloth, then glaze. Decorate with aspic jelly and creamed butter, forced through a pipe; substitute bits of truffle for the eyes and serve in the old-fashioned way: mouth stuffed apples and lemons, and ears sprigged with rosemary. Or put an orange in its mouth instead, and festoon with scarlet ribbons.

If preferred, you can substitute strips of tongue rolled up and alternated with strips of fat bacon for some of the force-meat in the head, or it can be used in veal and ham pies. In the olden days, the head was carried into the banqueting hall by the next in rank to the Lord of the Feast, preceded by a body of henchmen, and a fanfare of trumpets and placed first on the Christmas board. Now it sits in solemn state on the sideboard.

MIREPOIX FOR BOAR'S HEAD

Take half a pound of fat bacon, half a pound of lean ham, two scraped carrots, two peeled onions, four peeled mushrooms, three peeled shallots, a clove of garlic, three bay leaves, two laurel leaves, some sprigs of thyme, six cloves, two blades of mace and a teaspoonful of peppercorns. Chop bacon and ham, carrots, onions, mushrooms and shallots and place in a stew pan with three ounces of fresh butter, then add herbs, etc. Fry all to a golden brown colour. Now add two good glasses of Madeira or sherry, and a pint of excellent broth. Boil the *mirepoix* gently for about one and a half hours, and then strain it through a tammy, and use as directed.

HOTTE PEACOCKE *c.* 1500

PEACOCK IN HIS PRIDE

'This recipe was used by the cook of Henry the Seventh
at Her Royal Master's Coronation Banquet.' VICTORIA

The peacock, which was introduced to Britain by the
Romans, was always given the place of honour on Royal
tables at Christmas time. Sometimes as many as a hundred
birds were served at a single banquet. In olden days, cooks
held the belief that the peacock cried at night because he
could not see his own beauty and thought he had lost it. Another ancient belief was that peacocks fed on serpents which
was supposed to account for their animal cry.

TO DIGHT A PEACOCK

'Take and flay off the skin with the feathers and tail, leaving
the neck and crest still upon the bird, and preserving the flory
of his crest from injury when roasting by wrapping it in a
linen bandage. Then take the skin with all the feathers upon
it and spread it out on a table and sprinkle thereon ground
cinnamon. Now roast the peacocke and "endore" him with the
yolkes of many eggs, and when he is roasted remove him
from the fire and let him cool for a while. Then take and sew
him again into his skin and all his feathers, and remove the
bandage from his crest. Brush the feathers carefully and dust
upon them and his comb gilding to enhance his beauty. After
a while, set him upon a golden platter, garnish with rosemary
and other green leaves, and serve him forthwith as if he were
alive, and with great ceremony.'

ANOTHER WAY OF PREPARING THE KINGLY BIRD

'A peacocke may also have the skin and feathers removed as
described above when it may be stuffed with spices and sweet
herbs, and finely chopped savoury meats, and roasted as
described in the foregoing recipe. Then replace the skin and
feathers when it should be "served whole with the comb
entire and the tail spread to its widest and proudest extent".'
On grand occasions, when the King wished his feast to be

specially splendid, the tail of the peacock was covered with leaf of gold, and a piece of cotton dipped in spirits was put in its beak. This was set fire to as the bird was brought in Royal procession to table with musical honours.

The privilege of serving and distributing the 'Peacock in His Pride' was reserved for the Ladies of the Court of the highest birth, or for those distinguished by Royal favour for their beauty or wit.

THE PROCESSION OF THE PEACOCK

'When the Peacock was all arrayed in his "Pride", Royal trumpeters blowing on silver horns, or other musicians making "Sweet Musick", led the way to the banqueting hall followed by the First Lady carrying the Peacock and then by a bevy of maidens clad in white, and behind walked pages bearing the utensils needed for the carving of the Royal bird.

'The Lady as she proudly bore the Royal bird to its place of honour before the King, held it aloft "for all to see". The platter on which it rested could either be of gold or silver, but it is said that on one occasion, Queen Elizabeth wrecked the life and happiness of two of her courtiers because the dish on which the Royal bird was borne was of silver instead of gold. She was furious because she was entertaining the Duc d'Anjou at the moment, and wished to impress him with the magnificence of her court and her possessions. The silver dish irritated her beyond measure, and so, flying into a passion, she refused to sanction the marriage of the Lady who bore the Peacock into her august presence, with the gentleman who carried the sauce, and for nine dreary months declined to reconsider her refusal.

'At great Royal feasts, as many as one hundred and four Peacocks have been served at once.' c. 1500

SWANS

All the swans on the River Thames are owned partly by the Sovereign and partly by two city companies: the Vintners, who have what they call a 'swan feast' every spring, and the Dyers, who have theirs in the winter.

Until about fifty years ago, every year at the approach of Christmas, the King's swanmaster collected a number of young birds and penned them up 'to get the weed off them', feeding them on meal, etc. They were then killed and sent to the Royal table or as presents to the King's friends. This custom is now in abeyance.

VENISON STEW *c.* 1800

Take of venison, and cut into small pieces, and brown in hot butter in an earthen stewpan. Then add a quarter ounce of mace, a quarter ounce of cloves, a quarter ounce of cinnamon, a quarter ounce of Jamaica pepper, and a quarter ounce of black pepper, and a whole nutmeg. Pound all spices together before adding to stew, then add along with a pint of claret, and stew very slowly till tender. Serve with sippets of toast.

Only the leg and part of the saddle of venison is served at Royal tables. Venison should be kept a long time before cooking, and before 'hanging' it should be dredged with flour and pepper to keep flies and dust away. E.C.

PLUM PUDDING

Although it is said that Plum Pudding as known today, so beloved of George the Fourth, was not generally served till five years after the Battle of Waterloo, Plum Porridge, its predecessor, an offshoot of Plum Broth, was popular from the beginning of the sixteenth century, as a combined meat and pudding.

PLUM PORRIDGE OR PLUM POTTAGE
c. 1600

*An Old Royal Christmas Dish, the Forerunner
of Plum Pudding*

Take twelve quarts of extra good beef soup made from legs of beef. If very excellent soup is desired, add two ox tongues, put in soup fine whole bread sliced and crumbled, raisins, seeded, currants picked, and stoned prunes, of these two pounds each. Add lemons, mace and cloves, all boiled in a muslin bag in syrup, one quart of red wine and after boiling for half an hour, a pint of sack, brandy or Madeira wine. Put in a cool place and it will keep many weeks.

EMPIRE CHRISTMAS PUDDING

Created by Mr Henry Cédard, G.C.A., Maître Chef to His Majesty. Buckingham Palace, Christmas, 1927

> 5 lbs Australian currants
> 5 lbs Australian sultanas
> 5 lbs South African stoned raisins
> 1½ lbs minced Canadian apples
> 5 lbs United Kingdom breadcrumbs
> 5 lbs New Zealand beef suet
> 2 lbs South African cut candied peel
> 2½ lbs United Kingdom flour
> 2½ lbs West Indies Demerara sugar
> 20 eggs (Irish Free State)
> 2 ozs Ceylon ground cinnamon
> 1½ ozs Zanzibar ground cloves
> 1½ ozs ground nutmegs (Straits
>   Settlements)
> 1 teaspoon Indian pudding spice
> ¼ pint Cyprus brandy
> ½ pint Jamaica rum
> 2 quarts Old English Beer

PRINCESS ELIZABETH'S CHRISTMAS PUDDING *c.* 1946

> ½ lb cleaned currants
> ½ lb cleaned sultanas
> ½ lb chopped stoned raisins
> ½ lb shredded beef suet
> 3 ozs chopped candied peel
> ½ lb flour

½ lb breadcrumbs
6 ozs sugar
1 cup treacle
5 Australian eggs
Pinch of salt
Squeeze of lemon juice

Place fruit, suet, peel, flour, breadcrumbs and sugar in a basin.
Mix well. Heat treacle. Beat and stir in the eggs. Mix into
the dry ingredients with salt and lemon juice. Beat well. Press
into a greased pudding basin. Cover with buttered paper, then
with a scalded floured cloth. Steam for six hours.

ROYAL CHRISTMAS PUDDING *c.* 1565

'VIANDE ARDENTE'

¾ lb Malaga raisins
¾ lb sultanas
½ lb chopped peeled apples
¾ lb currants
1 lb chopped suet
½ lb sifted flour
2 ozs ground ginger
½ oz powdered cloves
½ oz powdered cinnamon
½ oz powdered nutmeg
½ lb powdered sugar
½ pint rum or brandy
Juice and chopped rind of ½ orange
    and ½ lemon
6 ozs breadcrumbs
3 ozs each of candied orange,
    lemon and citron peel
6 ozs chopped, blanched almonds
6 eggs
⅓ pint stout

Steep all the cleaned and prepared fruit in liqueur for twenty-

F

four hours, then thoroughly mix the whole. Pour into white earthenware basins, press firmly in, and wrap in a buttered and floured pudding cloth. Tie with a knot on top. Cook in boiling water or in steam for six hours at least. When required, cook again for six hours. To serve, sprinkle the pudding with heated brandy or rum and set alight.

King Edward the Seventh preferred his plum pudding moistened only with eggs and old English ale or beer instead of brandy, which royal cooks had been using since the days of William the Fourth. E.C.

VICTORIAN PLUM PUDDING *c.* 1845

5 beaten eggs
$\frac{1}{2}$ pint thick cream
1 teaspoon rosewater
5 tablespoons sifted flour
$\frac{3}{4}$ teaspoon salt
$\frac{1}{4}$ teaspoon ground mace
$\frac{1}{4}$ teaspoon grated nutmeg
$\frac{1}{2}$ teaspoon ground cinnamon
$\frac{1}{2}$ lb. castor sugar
$\frac{1}{2}$ gill brandy
$\frac{1}{2}$ gill white wine
$\frac{1}{2}$ lb shredded suet
6 ozs chopped raisins
$\frac{3}{4}$ lb currants
$\frac{1}{2}$ lb sieved breadcrumbs
Grated rind $\frac{1}{2}$ a lemon
2 ozs minced candied lemon peel

Beat eggs with cream till frothy. Stir in rose water, and flour sifted with salt and spices. When blended, stir in sugar, brandy and wine. Beat till into a smooth batter. Mix suet with raisins, currants, breadcrumbs and peels. Stir into flour, incorporating enough additional flour to make a dropable batter. Cover and stand for twelve hours. Three-quarters fill greased pudding basins. Cover with greased paper and pudding cloths. Steam for eight to ten hours.

A MERRY CHRISTMASTIDE

Drink now the strong Beere,
Cut the white loafe here,
The while the meat is a shredding:
For the rare Mince-Pie
And the Plums stand by
To fill the Paste that's a kneading.

ROBERT HERRICK

AN ANCIENT RECIPE FOR MINCEMEAT *c.* 1702

Take two pounds of the lean of the rump of beef, two pounds of fine beef suet, shredded very finely, and put to this three pounds of cleaned currants, two pounds of brown sugar, a pinch of salt, two ounces of powdered cinnamon and a large nutmeg grated. Mix altogether and put in glazed pots and tie down with a bladder. This will keep good for three months. When you use it, add to this quantity a pint of sack [sherry], half a pound mixed candied peel, the juice of two lemons and four fine, firm apples, pared and grated.

LEMON MINCE PIES *c.* 1825

Juice of two lemons, and rind boiled together till rind is tender. Pound it and add one pound of loaf sugar, suet chopped finely, a few spoonfuls of red wine, one pound of cleaned currants, three pounds of peeled apples, chopped, and a little brandy. Mix, adding spice to taste.

THE WASSAIL BOWLE

Sad as it may seem that no longer do the lady guests, 'most distinguished by birth or beauty' serve the lordly peacock, that 'pheasants drenched with amber grease' are not now offered as a *pièce de résistance,* and that we are now never asked to sample 'pies of carp's tongues', yet there is still the wassail bowl to drink and the Yule log to sample when its godfather is blazing on a Yuletide hearth.

TO MAKE A BOWLE OF WASSAILE
c. 1601

Wassail! Wassail! all over the town
Our toast it is white, our ale is brown;
Our bowl it is made of the maplin-tree,
We be good fellows all; I drink unto thee.

AN OLD GLOUCESTERSHIRE WASSAILERS' SONG

Boil a quarter ounce each of bruised ginger, cinnamon, nutmeg, and a couple each of cloves, corianders and cardamons in three-quarters of a tumblerful of water for ten minutes. Add a quart of ale, a bottle of sherry, and from half a pound to one pound of sugar. Heat, but do not get near the boiling-point. Then beat the yolks of six eggs and the whites of three eggs and throw them into a bowl. Slowly add half the heated ale and wine, stirring all the while. Bring the remainder to the boil, and pour it also into bowl. Lastly, throw into bowl six roasted apples which have been cored and stuffed with sugar, and drink to the old days when 'The Lord of Misrule' was king.

SNAPDRAGON *c.* 1560

For a Christmas Party

Place stalked muscatel raisins in a metal dish. Cover with brandy and set alight. Decorate dish with berried holly. Let the players snatch the raisins out of the flaming brandy.

MENUS

In King Henry the Eighth's day, heavy meals served from gold, silver, gilded or pewter dishes were the custom. A dinner menu usually consisted of:

¶ First Course: Potage or Stewed Broath, Boilede Meat or Stewed Meat, Chekeyns and Bacon, Powdred Beefe, Pyes, Goose, Pygge, Roosted Beefe, Roosted Vele, Custarde.

¶ Second Course: Roosted Lambe, Roosted Capons, Roosted Connies [rabbits:], Pehennes [pea hens], Baken Venison, Tarte.

The supper usually consisted of:

¶ First Course: Potage, a Sallette, a Pygge's Pettytoes, Powdred Beefe, Shoulder or Breste of Mutton, Vele, Lambe, Custarde.

¶ Second Course: Roosted Capons, Connies, Chekyns, Pigeons or Larkes, A Pye of Pigeons, or Chekyns, Baken Venison, Tarte.

In Elizabethan days, dinner menus were very elaborate. Her Majesty took a keen interest in the pleasures of the table.

MENUS FOR AN
ELIZABETHAN BANQUET

¶ FIRST COURSE: Wheaten Flummery, Spinach or Stewed Broath, Gruel or Hotch Potch.

¶ SECOND COURSE: Lampreys, Stock-fish, Sturgeon, etc. 'with side dishes of porpoises'.

¶ THIRD COURSE: Quaking Pudding, Black puddings, Marrow puddings, White puddings, etc.

¶ FOURTH COURSE: Beef, Capons, Game, Mutton, Marrow Pasties, Humble Pie, Scotch Collops, Wild Fowl, Etc.

¶ FIFTH COURSE: Cheese cakes, Various creams, Custardes, Jellies, Junkets, Syllabubs, Warden Pies, etc. followed by White Cheese and Fancy cake.

Ale and beer, sack and Bordeaux, Burgundy and Rhenish wine and different varieties of mead or metheglin, some of which were concocted from as many as twenty-five herbs, were served at a banquet of this kind.

LORD MAYOR'S BANQUET

This banquet at The Guildhall was honoured by the presence of King George the Third and Queen Charlotte in 1791.

¶ FIRST SERVICE: Otto Turtle Pottages, John Dories, Red Mullet, etc. Roast Venison, Westphalia Hams. Poulets à la Royale. Tongues Espagniole. Chickens à la Reine. Tondron Devaux à la Danzie. Harrico. Popiets of Veal Glasse. Fillets of Lamb à la Condé. Comports of Squabs. Fillets of Beef Marinate. Mutton à la Memorance. Fine Vegetables.

¶ SECOND SERVICE: Ortolans. Quails. Wheat Ears. Goodevan Patte. Perrigoe Pye. Pea Chicks. Woodcocks. Pheasants. Teal. Snipe. Partridge. Pattys Royal.

¶ THIRD SERVICE: Ragout Royal. Green Morells. Green Peas. Fine Fat Liver. Fine Combs. Green Truffles. Artichokes à la Provinciale. Mushrooms au Blank. Cardons à la Benjamel. Knots of Eggs. Ducks' Tongues. Peths. Truffles in Oil. Pallets. Ragout Mille.

¶ FOURTH SERVICE: Curious Ornamental Cakes. Blomanges, representing different figures. Clear Marbrays. Cut Pastry. Mille Fuelles.

Centre of Table: Grand Pyramid of Demies of various Shell Fish. Various Cold Viands are: Temples, Shapes, Landscapes in Jellies. Savoury Cakes. Almond Gothes. Grand Epergnes filled with Fine Pickles, Laspicks, Rolards, etc.

When the banquet was over, following the usual tradition, the loving cups (tall golden goblets) were passed round. Three people always stood during this solemn rite: the man who had just drunk, the one receiving the cup and about to drink, and a third who stood immediately behind the guest who was raising the goblet to his lips. The necessity for the third person no longer exists, and the custom which survived for centuries is now abolished. Today, when Royalty is present at the Guildhall, the Royal guests and all the other distinguished guests at the head table, rise to their feet and keep upstanding while the loving cup is passed round.

MENU FOR ROYAL PRINCES' BALL
1820

SERVICE CHAUD

Ris au Lait d'Amandes
Rissoles de Légumes
Filets de Volaille
Sagou au Consommé

Bouchées à la Béchamel
Côtelettes d'Agneau à la
Purée de Marrons

SERVICE FROID

Petits Canetons de Volaille
 à la Gelée
Sandwiches Variés
Arbre en Nougat, portant
 des Fruits Glacés
Poisson en Gâteau-punch
Paniers d'Orange à la Gelée

Galantines de Mauviettes
Petits-pains à la Française
Croquembouch Orné de
 Sucre Filé
Jambon Imité à la Gelée
Charlotte Russe
Pôts de Cremê au Chocolat

CORBEILLES DE FRUIT

Assiettes Montées, Garnies
 de Bonbons

Tambours, Garnis de Petits
 Fours

DUKE OF WELLINGTON'S FAVOURITE DINNER c. 1816

Written in Queen Victoria's own Handwriting

Clear Soup

Boiled Turbot

Anchovy Sauce

Neck of Venison

Young Ducks with Young Green Peas
Served with Butter and Without Mint

Roast Chicken
with
Bread Sauce flavoured with Parsley

Gooseberry Tart
(or Cherry or Red Currant Tart made into 'short
pastry' with whipped cream unflavoured)
Strawberries
(when in season served with fine sugar)
Bordeaux Wine

*The Duke of Wellington lost his best cook because he cared so little
about what he had to eat. E.C.*

QUEEN VICTORIA'S CHRISTMAS DINNER

Osborne, December, 1895

Purée of Celery à la Crême
Cream of Rice à l'Indienne
Purée of Pheasant à la Chasseur
Soles Frites
Sauce aux Anchois
Woodcocks à la Robert
Quenelles of Fowls à l'Essence
Salmis of Widgeon à la Bigarade
Border of Rice garnished with a Purée of Pheasant
Filet de Boeuf
Roast Turkey à la Périgord
Roast Goose à l'Anglaise
Faisans.   Gélinottes
Plum Pudding
Mince Pies à l'Anglaise
Pudding à la Gotha
Pudding de Cabinet
Nougats de Pommes
Tourte de Pommes à la Coburg
Gelée de Citron

ON THE SIDEBOARD

Boar's Head
Baron of Beef
Woodcock Pie

WINES

Sherry or Amontillado
Dry White Wines
Champagne and Moselle
Burgundy and Bordeaux

F*

Malmsey-Madeira
Liqueurs
Port, Sherry, Madeira and Claret
(Balmoral Whisky and Apollinaris for the use
of Her Majesty who takes nothing else.)

YACHTING DINNER AT COWES

Given by His Majesty King Edward the Seventh on
H.M.Y. *Victoria and Albert, Cowes. August 4th,* 1909

Tortue Claire
Blanchailles au Naturel et Diablées
Chaudfroid de Volaille à la Russe
Selle d'Agneau à la Chivry
Dindonneaux et Cailles Rôtis
Artichauts, Sauce Hollandaise
Mousseline de Fruits au Grand Marnier
Croutes de Jambon à la Windsor
Glace à la Circassienne

LUNCHEON AT WINDSOR CASTLE

Given by His Majesty King George the Fifth.
Windsor Castle, June 14th, 1911

Consommé Belle Fermière
Crabe
Sauce Rémoulade
Côtelettes de Mouton à la Reforme
Poulets Rôtis
Les Viandes Froides
Salade
Quartier d'Artichauts à l'Italienne
Pannequets Soufflés
Tarte aux Cerises

CORONATION EVE DINNER

Given by their Majesties King George the Fifth and Queen Mary on the eve of their Coronation. *Buckingham Palace, June 19th,* 1911

Tortue Claire
Filets de Truite à l'Hotelière
Suprèmes de Volaille Grosvenor
Selle d'Agneau à la Florian
Cailles Rôties
Asperges
Sauce Mousseline
Pêches Mazarin
Kirsch de Lorraine
Biscuits Glacés Princesse

CORONATION BANQUET

Mr Henry Cédard, G.C.A., Maître Chef to His Majesty. *Buckingham Palace, June 20th,* 1911

Tortue Claire
Filets de Sole Britannia
Canetons à l'Imperial
Selles d'Agneau Princière
Cailles à la Royale flanquées d'Ortolans
Asperges d'Argenteuil
Sauce Chantilly
Pêches à la George V
Pâtisserie Variée
Cassolettes à l'Aurore
Mousses de Fraises Reine Mary
Bonbonnières de Friandises
Gaufrettes

CORONATION BALL SUPPER

Buckingham Palace, June 20th, 1911

Consommé Froid

Medaillons de Truits à la Norvégienne
Chaudfroid de Cailles à la Bohemiènne
Poulets Découpés Garnis de Langue

Petits Pains à la Strasbourgeoise
Sandwiches Variés

Macedoine de Fruits au Champagne
Gelée aux Fraises

Pâtisserie sur Socles
Paniers de Friandises

Orangeade   Limonade
Dessert

DINNER MENU

Mr Henry Cédard, G.C.A., Maître Chef to His Majesty.
Holyrood Palace, July 20th, 1911

Consommé à l'Orleans

Filets de Soles Frits Doria

Mousseline d'Ortolans à la Lucullus

Selles d'Agneau à la Nivernaise

Filets de Boeuf Froids Bouquetière

Dindonneaux Rôtis Flanqués de Cailles

Asperges
Sauce Chantilly

Pêches Pompadour
Petits Gateaux

Kirsch de Lorraine

Coupes Sienna Morenna
Paniers de Friandises

Gaufrettes

ROYAL STATE DINNER

DURBAR DAY

Mr Henry Cédard, G.C.A., Maître Chef to His Majesty.
Delhi. December 12th, 1911

Tortue
Consommé à l'Ancienne Froid
Filets de Becti à la Nantua
Cailles à la Gastronome
Selle d'Agneau à l'Anglaise
Dindonneaux et Perdreaux Rôtis
Asperges
Sauce Mousseline
Pêches à la Reine Marie
Barquettes à l'Indienne
Biscuits George V
Friandises

EMPIRE DINNER

Composed by the Chef de Cuisine to the Prince of Wales

Plovers' Eggs
Clear Soup with Vegetables
Fillet of Trout Sauté
Parsley or Fine Herb Sauce
Braised Sweetbread
Green Peas   New Potatoes
Roast Spring Chicken with Bacon
Potato Chips   Green Salad
Asparagus
Cream Sauce
Soufflé of Lemon
Soft Herring Roes on Toast

PRINCESS ROYAL'S WEDDING BREAKFAST

Mr Henry Cédard, G.C.A., Maître Chef to His Majesty.
Buckingham Palace, February 26th, 1922

The menu, which was ornamented with a pink and gold border in which bloomed the rose, the shamrock, and the thistle, emblems of England, Ireland and Scotland, had the monograms of the King and Queen emblazoned at the head, and those of Princess Mary and Viscount Lascelles at the foot.

Consommé Soubrette

Filets de Sole à la Reine

Côtelettes d'Agneau à la Princesse
Petits Pois

Chaudfroid de Poularde à la Harewood

Langue or Jambon Découpés
Salade Caprice

Timbales de Gaufres à la Windsor

Friandises

Dessert

Café

DUKE OF YORK'S WEDDING BREAKFAST

Buckingham Palace, 1923

Consommé à la Windsor

Suprêmes de Saumon, Reine Mary

Côtelettes d'Agneau, Prince Albert

Chapons à la Strathmore

Jambon et Langue Découpés à l'Aspic
Salade Royale

Asperges
Sauce Crême Mousseuse

Fraises, Duchesse Elizabeth
Panier de Friandises
Dessert
Café

HIS MAJESTY'S LUNCHEON AT ASCOT RACES

Mr Henry Cédard, G.C.A., Maître Chef to His Majesty.
Ascot, June 18th, 1924

Medaillons de Truite Epicurienne
Mignonnettes d'Agneau Princesse
Chaudfroid de Poulet Andalouse
Buffet
Derby Beef Jambon Langue
Roast Beef Agneau Sauce Menthe
Pigeon Pies Mutton Pies
Petits Pois et Pommes Nouvelles

Asperges Chantilly
Salade Printanier

Macedoine de Fruits
Pâtisserie des Gaufrettes

ROYAL STATE DINNER

Mr Henry Cédard, G.C.A., Maître Chef to His Majesty.
Buckingham Palace, July 14th, 1924

Consommé Carmen, Chaud et Froid
Medaillons de Truite, Saumonée Medicis
Cailles Nappées Infante
Côtelettes d'Agneau Belle Hélène
Poulardes Rôties
Salade
Soufflé Glacé à l'Espagnole
Friandises
Feuillantines au Fromage

CHRISTMAS LUNCHEON MENU
Sandringham, 1936

Mock Turtle Soup
Norfolk Turkey
Sandringham Beef
Yorkshire Pudding
Asparagus   Parsnips
Baked Potatoes   French Beans
Brussels Sprouts
Plum Pudding
Mince Pies   Ice Cream
Cheese   Biscuits   Celery
Fresh Fruit
Coffee

STATE BANQUET
Buckingham Palace, March 21st, 1939

Public banquet in honour. of the President of the French
Republic and Madame Lebrun

Consommé Quenelles aux Trois Couleurs
Filet de Truite Saumonée Roi George VI
Rouennais à la Gelée Reine Elizabeth
Garniture Buzancy
Mignonnette d'Agneau Royale
Petits Pois à la Française
Pommes Nouvelles Rissolées au Beurre
Poussin Mercy-le-Haut
Salade Elysee
Asperges Vertes
Sauce Maltaise
Bombe l'Entente Cordiale
Corbeille Lorraine
Cassolette Bassillac

The Wines

Sherry 1865
Madeira Sercial 1834
Piesporter Goldtropfchen 1924
Deideshiemer Kieselberg 1921
Perrier-Jouet 1919
Chateau Haut Brion 1904
Chateau Yquem 1921
Port Royal Tawny
Port 1912
Brandy, 1815

DINNER GIVEN BY KING GEORGE THE FIFTH

Mr Henry Cédard, G.C.A., Maître Chef to His Majesty
Cowes, August 4th, 1924

Consommé Britannia

Suprèmes de Sole au Champagne

Côtelettes d'Agneau Valenciennes

Chapons Rôtis
Petits Pois à l'Anglaise

Coupes de pèches, Caprice
Charlotte Russe

Toast Laponien

FROM ROYAL STILLROOMS

In the olden days Royalty did not have to depend on Bond Street and other smart shopping districts in London and in Paris for toilet waters and other cosmetics. These were concocted in Royal stillrooms, as you will see from the receipts I am giving. The Royal scrap book also included receipts for homely cures for almost every ailment. Perhaps some of them may prove of interest to readers.

LAVENDER WATER

Copied in Queen Victoria's own handwriting and dated, 1836

Put a quart of Spring water to every pound of freshly picked lavender flowers, and distill it very slowly in a cold still. Put into a pot till all is distilled. Then clean the still very well out. Add the lavender water and distill it off as slowly as possible. Bottle and cork closely.

FOR A SORE BREAST *c.* 1773

Take half a pound of mutton suet, where the kidneys lie, and after it is well dried up put upon it in a mortar half a pound of the best yellow beeswax, and two ounces each of frankincense and white rosin powdered. Set them on the fire, stirring all the while till melted, then pour into a well-glazed pot. When required, dip some thin linen cloths into the mixture and apply.

POT POURRI *c.* 1839

Take a peck of roses gathered in the morning as soon as the dew is off them. Pick them clean from the green, but be careful not to lose the yellow seeds as they are the sweetest part. Take one pound of common salt, two ounces of bay salt, one ounce of saltpetre, one ounce of pimiento, and half an ounce each of cloves and cinnamon. Let your spices be well pounded, and the salt also and well mixed together. Put a layer of rose leaves into a deep jar, and sprinkle them with the salt and spice till you have put in all your roses. Stir every day for a fortnight, adding a few roses each day. Then put to it a dozen bay leaves and a handful of lavender flowers. You may mix blossoms and clove pinks with the roses if you like, and sixpenny worth of musk, if obtainable. Be careful that no green of any sort be in it except the bay leaves nor any white roses.

The lavender should be cut before the blossoms are fully open. Dry in a cool, airy room. I would also add some dried sprigs of lemon verbena, dried rosemary and dried marjoram, and a handful of dried leaves of balm of Gilead. The best way to dry leaves is to spread them on a fine sieve so that the air circulates round them. E.C.

SALINE DRAUGHT *c.* 1850

> 2 drachms of carbonate of potash
> 18 tablespoons water
> 4 knots of sugar

Mix these in a bottle and, when a saline draught is wanted, pour three tablespoonfuls into a tumbler and add a tablespoon of lemon juice.

SYRUP OF MARSHMALLOWS *c.* 1816

A small glass each of oil of almonds, and marshmallows mixed with half a nutmeg grated. Take before going to bed in a glass of mountain wine.

SENNA TEA *c.* 1841

Two ounces of senna leaves boiled in a quart of water and allowed to simmer all night by the fire. Be sure to have all the stalks picked out. When cold, add one ounce of tincture of senna. Take of this mixture about two or three tablespoons at any time when required. Cork it down and it will keep for some time.

VIOLET DRINK *c.* 1818

*As taken by Her Royal Highness, the Duchess of Kent,
Mother of Queen Victoria*

One teaspoonful of dried violetts and a half pint of boyling water. Infuse for six minutes and sweeten with honey. To cure pain and soothe the system under attacks of bronchitis, fevers and catarrhs.

ROSE LEAF DRINK *c.* 1650

THE ORIGINAL RECEIPT OF QUEEN HENRIETTA MARIA

Infuse one part of red rose leaves and a cup of boiling water. The rose leaves should half fill the cup. Leave upon the fire for ten minutes, then take off and strain and sweeten with honey and drink cold and fasting. Females only should drink this concoction.

CAMOMILE TEA *c.* 1836

QUEEN ADELAIDE'S RECIPE

Two dozen camomile flowers infused in one pint of boiling water for half an hour. Strain, sweeten with honey, and drink half a gill, fasting. A cure for indigestion, and for the ails of females.

VIOLET SYRUP *c.* 1856

AS COOKED FOR QUEEN VICTORIA

Take eight ounces of dried perfumed violets, one pound of fine loaf sugar, one ounce of picked gum arabic, melted in a quarter pint of hot water, and one drachm of powdered orris root. Put a copper pot containing the violets upon a charcoal stone fire and add the orris root. Pour in water slowly and carefully. Boil for ten minutes. Squeeze out through a clean muslin cloth into a basin. Add sugar and gum arabic and some drops of cochineal. Boil to remove scum. When cold, bottle. Good for lung trouble.

AN EXCELLENT TOOTH CLEANSER

Victoria, May 1st, 1835

Mix two ounces of Peruvian bark with two ounces of myrrh, one ounce of powdered chalk, and one ounce of orris root.

TO CURE TOOTHACHE

'*As told me by my Grand-aunt.' Victoria. May 2nd,* 1835

Take of alum, reduced to powder, two drachms, nitrous spirits of ether five drachms, mix and apply to the painful member.

CURE FOR AN ILL SKIN *c.* 1569

OINTMENT ORIGINALLY MADE FOR MARY, QUEEN OF SCOTS

This was copied by Queen Victoria into her scrap book, and copied several times by other people, ladies-in-waiting and women-in-attendance, in two or three little note-books kept by her Royal Highness.

'Mix and intermingle four parts of single oyle of almonds with four parts of the oyle of ye whale or of pigg or of the cream fatt of milk (the whale's oyle be ye best). Put thereto four ounces of damask [red rose] water, and mix together with a silver spoon and make fine and smoothe.'

ANOTHER FAIRE UNJUENT MADE FOR THE QUEEN'S MAJESTIE 1567–1635

It is uncertain who was the queen referred to—probably Mary, Queen of Scots, but it may have been Queen Henrietta Maria.

Take of olive oyle one and a half parts, one part of oyle of whales or of pigg's fatt, one part of virgin's wax, one part of camphor, two parts fresh honey. Place all in a silver dish, and place this dish within a saucepan holding therein hott water, and sett either by the fire or within an open oven to remain there until dissolved. Stir then the whole together and dropp therein the perfume of damask water and stir till very cold.

FOR WEAK NERVES

Drink much scull cap tea and avoid excitement. VICTORIA. *May 2nd, 1836*

TO CURE A SORE THROAT *c.* 1829

Gargle with a mixture of one teaspoonful of cayenne, two teaspoonfuls of fine salt, and a small cup of water, and take a draught of pepper sauce. Also chew white pond lily root.

A FINE WHOLESOME OINTMENT FOR BLISTERS, BITES OF FLEAS AND OTHER INSECTS *c.* 1575

Take of oyle of scorpions two ounces, hedgehogge's greese one ounce, badger's greese one ounce, bear's greese one ounce, good sallett oyle half a pint, red lead six ounces, white lead seven ounces, all finely ground. Lay upon a linen cloth and apply to the spot.

THE QUEEN MAJESTIE'S CURE FOR PAIN IN YE EYES AND HEAD, ALSO FOR YE RHEUM *c.* 1689

Take nettles, elder leaves and bruise them into a very little bay salt, sprinkle a little *Aqua Vitae* along with these, and some pepper. Warm and lay to the nape of ye neck. If it be winter take ground ivy and use it as aforesaid. This be the ivy which do run along the earth, which is lesser leaved than the other kinds of ivy.

TO KEEP THE LIPS SOFT AND REDD
c. 1703

Take of equal portions—spirit, tincture of redd roses, the mucilage of quince seeds and virgin wax. Place all in a clean gallipot covered with a lid, and putt in a small stewpan and allow to steep gently by the side of the fire for ten minutes. Perfume with essence of roses, lavender, or rosemary. Make cold and put upon the skin.

'HOW MY WARTS WERE CURED' *c.* 1815
THE PRINCESS CHARLOTTE'S OWN RECIPE

Take of bruised leaves of the *calendula officinalis* and blend with weak vinegar.

'A RECEIPT GIVEN TO ME BY MY AUNT TO IMPROVE MY TEETH'
Victoria, 1835

White teeth are a great addition to beauty. The following wash will help to preserve them in good condition. With a quart of fresh rain water, mix the juice of a lemon, six ounces burnt alum and six ounces of cooking salt. Boil this for one minute in a cup, then strain and place in a bottle for future use. Rub this wash upon the teeth with a small sponge tied to a small stick thrice a week.

TO MAKE HAIR GROW (i) *c.* 1837

Take southernwood and burn to ashes and mix with sweet oil and rub scalp.

Southernwood (Artemisia Abortanum) *is a fragrant cottage garden plant known in some parts of Britain as 'Lads' Love'. and in others as 'Old Man'. This plant thrives in light well-drained ordinary soil in a sunny position. Plant roots in September, October or March. I have often rooted cuttings of this shrub in a jar of water. E.C.*

TO MAKE HAIR GROW (ii) *c.* 1653

Beat three tablespoonfuls of honey well with a handful of vine sprigs that twist like wire. Strain the juice into the honey. Anoint the bald places therewith.

FOR ILL NERVES *c.* 1834

Hyssop: Steep a quarter ounce of dried hyssop flowers in a pint of boiling water for ten minutes. Sweeten with honey. Take a wineglassful three times a day for lung trouble.

FOR A SORE MOUTH *c.* 1678

Take elder water, red rose water, rose leaves infused in it, and claret wine. Put all together of each a like quantity, and put therein honey and stirr together. Warm the sauce and wash the mouth with it.

CURE FOR SHINGLES *c.* 1700

Take juice of garden herbs, mints, grass of each a like quantity, put to it sallett oyle, not so much as to make it appear green, and put thereto as much white wyne and vinegar as of juice and oyle, a handful of dry salt beaten small, and with a feather annoint ye shingles morning and evening.

TO MAKE YOU SLEEP *c.* 1685

Take ye juice of ground ivy, put to it a little white of an egg, dipp flax into it and ty to your temples and bind it.

FOR A BLISTER, A SORE, A SCALDE
c. 1657

Take of bays, brambles, half a handful of each, of dog mint a good handful, of ground ivy half a handful. Choppe well together, and boyle them a good while in mutton suett and a little hogg's skin and keep a whole year. Both greeses must be rough. Spread it upon a fine cloth of linen, and put upon the place two times in the day and night.

FOR A COLD OR RHEUM *c.* 1833

Add thirty drops of sal volatile (camphorated) to a small wineglassful of warm water.

RULES FOR PRESERVING THE HEALTH OF THE BODY

'Which if diseased or ill-conditioned affects the indwelling soul.' Victoria, June, 1835

Never sit up late. Never stay in bed late in the morning. Sponge the entire body every morning with cold spring water. This should be done at once upon rising. Dry with a rough towel and continue to friction the skin of the whole person for not less than fifteen minutes every day.

Drink four large half pint tumblers of clear cold, or very hot water each day upon an empty stomach. That is to say, upon rising, at about 11 a.m., at 2.30 p.m. and at bed-time.

Take a corrective digestive dose of medicine once in each week.

Sleep with the window open at the top—even in wet or cold weather.

Keep the head cool by washing it frequently in cold water and avoid nervousness by resting often.

MORE RULES FOR HEALTH

Eat sparingly. Three meals a day are enough. More are injurious.

Never indulge in dainty foods between meals.

Avoid sweetmeats.

Fruit is most beneficial to the system.

Never eat a heavy supper, especially of animal food, shortly before going to bed, and drink wine or beer only with or after a meal.

Keep the feet warm and dry, and the head cool, and the digestive organs open and a doctor will be rarely required.

MANNERS FOR A YOUNG LADY OF HIGH BIRTH

Blush when modesty requires you to blush—it is becoming in a young female. Forbear to speak loudly. If it should be that a history of scandal unbecoming to maidenly ears be related or a joke be spoken which is not seemly, be discreet. Drop your eyelids and give no impression that you have even heard of the same. Be dignified in carriage and never affect languishing airs.

Control your appetite. Be not indelicate, be affable, be prudent and not a coquette.

GLOSSARY

amulet: *omelet*

ashet: *meat platter*

coffyns of pastrie: *pastry cases*

dight, to: *to prepare*

endore, to: *to coat or gild*

hoop: *baking tin*

mary-bones: *marrow bones*

neat: *ox or cow*

passed: *strained*

pipkin: *fireproof dish*

receipt: *recipe*

sack: *sherry*

sheet, to: *to line*

soppe: *slice of hot buttered toast
     with crust removed*

tossing pan: *frying pan*

verjus: *vinegar*

whitened: *blanched*

Also of interest from Hippocrene . . .

TRADITIONAL RECIPES FROM OLD ENGLAND

Arranged by country, this charming classic features the favorite dishes and mealtime customs from across England, Scotland, Wales and Ireland.

128 pages • 5 x 8 1/2 • 0-7818-0489-2 •W • $9.95pb • (157)

TRADITIONAL FOOD FROM SCOTLAND: THE EDINBURGH BOOK OF PLAIN COOKERY RECIPES

A delightful assortment of Scottish recipes and helpful hints for the home—this classic volume offers a window into another era.

336 pages • 5 1/2 x 8 • 0-7818-0514-7 • W • $11.95pb • (620)

TRADITIONAL FOOD FROM WALES

Bobby Freeman

Welsh food and customs through the centuries. This book combines over 260 authentic, proven recipes with cultural and social history

332 pages • 5 1/2 x 8 1/2 • 0-7818-0527-9 • NA • $24.95hc • (638)

CELTIC COOKBOOK: Traditional Recipes from the Six Celtic Lands Brittany, Cornwall, Ireland, Isle of Man, Scotland and Wales

Helen Smith-Twiddy

This collection of over 160 recipes from the Celtic world includes traditional, yet still popular dishes like Rabbit Hoggan and Gwydd y Dolig (Stuffed Goose in Red Wine).

200 pages•5 1/2 x 8 1/2 •0-7818-0579-1•NA•$22.50hc • (679)

THE ART OF IRISH COOKING
Monica Sheridan
Nearly 200 recipes for traditional Irish fare.
166 pages • 5 1/2 x 8 1/2 • 0-7818-0454-X • W • $12.95pb • (335)

GOOD FOOD FROM AUSTRALIA
Graeme and Betsy Newman
A generous sampling of over 150 Australian culinary favorites. "Steak, Chops, and Snags," "Casseroles and Curries," and "Outback Cooking" are among the intriguing sections included. In time for the 2000 Olympics in Sydney!
284 pages • 5 1/2 x 8 1/2 • 0-7818-0491-4 • W • $24.95hc • (440)

BEST OF AUSTRIAN CUISINE
Elisabeth Mayer-Browne
Nearly 200 recipes from Austria's rich cuisine: roasted meats in cream sauces, hearty soups and stews, tasty dumplings, and, of course, the pastries and cakes that remain Vienna's trademark.
224 pages • 5 x 8 1/2 • 0-7818-0526-0 • W • $11.95pb •(633)

A BELGIAN COOKBOOK
Juliette Elkon
A celebration of the regional variations found in Belgian cuisine.
224 pages • 5 1/2 x 8 1/2 • 0-7818-0461-2 • W • $12.95pb • (535)

ART OF DUTCH COOKING
C. Countess van Limburg Stirum
This attractive volume of 200 recipes offers a complete cross section of Dutch home cooking, adapted to American kitchens. A whole chapter is devoted to the Dutch Christmas, with recipes for unique cookies and candies that are a traditional part of the festivities.
192 pages•5 1/2 x 8 1/2 •illustrations •0-7818-0582-1•W•$11.95pb (683)

BEST OF SCANDINAVIAN COOKING: DANISH, NORWEGIAN AND SWEDISH

Shirley Sarvis and Barbara Scott O'Neil

This exciting collection of 100 recipes, each dish the favorite of a Scandinavian cook, spans the range of home cooking—appetizers, soups, omelets, pancakes, meats and pastries.

142 pages • 5 x 8 1⁄2 • 0-7818-0547-3 • W • $9.95pb • (643)

THE BEST OF FINNISH COOKING

Taimi Previdi

Two hundred easy to follow recipes covering all courses of the meal, along with menu suggestions and cultural background for major holidays and festivities such as Mayday and Midsummer.

242 pages • 5 x 8 1⁄2 Bilingual index • 0-7818-0493-0 • W • $12.95pb • (601)

THE BEST OF SMORGASBORD COOKING

Gerda Simonson

The traditional Swedish smorgasbord, a large table of hot and cold dishes, is meant to be a selection of appetizers before a seated dinner. Includes recipes for meat and game dishes, aspics and salads, fish, pastas and vegetables.

158 pages • 5 1⁄2 x 8 1⁄2 • 0-7818-0407-8 • W • $14.95pb • (207)

GOOD FOOD FROM SWEDEN

Inga Norberg

This classic of Swedish cookery includes recipes for fish and meat dishes, vegetables, breads and sweets, including cookies, cakes, candies and syrups.

192 pages • 5 x 8 1⁄2 • 0-7818-0486-8 • W • $10.95pb • (544)

ALL ALONG THE DANUBE: Recipes from Germany, Austria, Czechoslovakia, Yugoslavia, Hungary, Romania, and Bulgaria

Marina Polvay

For novices and gourmets, this unique cookbook offers a tempting variety of Central European recipes from the shores of the Danube River, bringing Old World flavor to today's dishes.

349 pages • 5 1/2 x 8 1/2 • 0-7818-0098-6 • W • $14.95pb • (491)

BAVARIAN COOKING

Olli Leeb

With over 300 recipes, this lovely collector's item cookbook covers every aspect of Bavarian cuisine from drinks, salads and breads to main courses and desserts.

"*Bavarian Cooking* is what a good regional cookbook should be—a guide for those who wish to know the heart and soul of a region's cooking, a book that anchors its recipes in the culture that produced them, and a cookbook that brings delight to the casual reader as well as to the serious cook ."

—*German Life*

176 pages • 6 1/2 x 8 1/4 • 0-7818-0561-9 • NA • $25.00 • (659)

THE SWISS COOKBOOK
Nika Standen Hazelton

Drawing from her long experience of and affection for Switzerland, cookbook expert Nika Hazelton explains the basic elements of Swiss cooking as it is understood and practiced in Swiss homes. Her "lessons" include such necessities as complete directions for "au bleu" fish cookery, for making superb dumplings or Swiss pasta, for plain or fancy Fondue in all its variations, and for roasting veal in the Swiss manner. The book's 250 recipes, gathered over many years from peasants, housewives, and chefs through history, cover the range of home cooking, from appetizers to desserts, all adapted for the American kitchen. Included are such delights as Heidi's Devil's Dip, Gypsy Salad, Farina-Cheese Soufflé, Minced Veal Bellevoir, and Apfelbröisi. This classic guide to Swiss cuisine, originally published by Atheneum, is sure to prove a favorite to today's cook as well.

236 pages • 5 ½ x 8 ½ • 0-7818-0587-2 • W • $11.95pb • (726)

WORLD'S BEST RECIPES

From Hippocrene's best-selling international cookbooks, comes this unique collection of culinary specialties from many lands. With over 150 recipes, this wonderful anthology includes both exotic delicacies and classic favorites from nearly 100 regions and countries. Sample such delights as Zambian Chicken Stew, Polish Apple Cake, Colombian Corn Tamales, Maltese Grouper with Artichokes, and Persian Pomegranate Khoreshe.

200 pages • 5 ½ x 8 ½ • 0-7818-0599-6 • W • $9.95pb • (685)